Acknowledgements

We wish to thank Goldsmiths' College, University of London, for providing the funds which facilitated a research project into clients' successful and unsuccessful experiences in counselling and psychotherapy. We are also extremely grateful to those people who allowed us to interview them and to learn from their views on therapy.

We are grateful to Chris Barker, Nancy Pistrang and David Shapiro for permission to reproduce the 'Opinions About Psychological Problems Questionnaire: Help for Psychological Problems' (Appendix 1).

Contents

Preface

We have both been deeply involved in counselling and psycho-therapy for many years. Our interest in writing this book has stemmed naturally from our immersion in the subject. We have in recent years been especially interested in trying to learn from the experiences of people who have had counselling and psycho-therapy. Fortunately, we have been able, with financial assistance from Goldsmiths' College, University of London, to interview a number of people who were willing to share their experiences of successful and unsuccessful counselling and psychotherapy so that we might learn what goes well and what goes wrong. Having previously edited a book which sought to identify various intellectual critiques of psychotherapy (*Psychotherapy and Its Discontents*) we wished in the present book to bring our learning to bear on the more pressing and practical concerns facing consumers.

There can be no doubt that a large number of people each year seek counselling and psychotherapy in Britain; it is impossible to know how many. We know from experience that it is difficult for anyone to find their way around the maze of therapies and to find their way to the kind of counsellor who will best be able to help them. Yet it becomes ever more important that people who are distressed or in need of psychological help should have guidance in finding such help.

In spite of criticisms of therapy, demand increases year by year. The provision of counselling in GPs' surgeries and other settings is gradually being extended. At the same time, there is a rightful pressure on therapists and counsellors to account for themselves ethically, theoretically, and clinically. Consumers have a vital role to play in putting pressure on helping professionals to explain themselves in accessible language, and to put their houses in order generally.

Our belief is that you would do well not to be drawn into fast decisions by the impressive names, claims, and qualifications paraded by practitioners in these fields. What follows in this book is based on our own experiences as consumers of counselling and psychotherapy; as trainers and supervisors of counsellors and psychotherapists; and as students of the process of helping people to discuss and resolve their innermost concerns. It is important for you to become sufficiently familiar with the central issues to be able to make informed choices. A certain amount of what we present here is based on research we have conducted with both satisfied and dissatisfied clients of counselling and psychotherapy. We are convinced that it is more important to listen to people's experiences and views than to rely on theory in order to find out what is most helpful in alleviating personal distress and achieving greater satisfaction in life.

We have made both direct and indirect use of what we have learnt from the people we have interviewed. Much of what follows is based on our inferences of what would have helped those interviewed to receive better counselling. We have also drawn on our own experiences and on the literature on counselling and psychotherapy. We hope we have for the most part avoided unnecessary jargon.

Included at the back of the book are references to some of the books cited in the text, as well as suggested reading. (When you come across references in the text (e.g. Dinnage, 1988), you can locate the full details at the end of the book.) We have also included a list of organizations providing counselling, psychotherapy, or pertinent information. As well as there being hundreds of different kinds of therapy, there are of course a number of books claiming to guide you through them! We hope that we have provided a balanced and useful account of the most important issues to consider before you embark on your therapeutic journey.

Our own view is that counselling and psychotherapy are largely identical activities, and for that reason we use the terms 'counselling', 'psychotherapy', and 'therapy' interchangeably throughout. We have also used the terms 'counsellor' and 'therapist', and 'patient' and 'client' interchangeably.

1
What is Counselling and Psychotherapy?

You may be extremely well-informed before beginning therapy or counselling, or you may have only the barest of ideas and impressions. We believe that it is wise to approach counselling and therapy as a consumer, as you would any other products and services. In considering parting with a great deal, or even a modest amount, of money, and engaging in a potentially life-changing contract, you will want to do some research of your own. By research, we mean anything from simply asking friends and neighbours about local mental health services, to reading extensively, participating in evening classes, and conducting your own 'survey'. Of course, the more acute and urgent your distress, the less likely will be your desire to assess objectively what is on offer. We do not want to foster the idea that help-seeking be delayed until a veritable portfolio of information is collected! In the case of severe distress, you are probably far better off turning to the most immediately available help than trying to evaluate all the pros and cons of therapy first.

In this chapter we aim to explain as well as we can what counselling is, what psychotherapy is, and what each of the other main helping activities resembling therapy are.

In the last ten years or so there has been rapid growth in the number of counsellors and psychotherapists, counselling and therapy organizations, and training courses. The public has heard a great deal about counselling through television, magazines, and newspapers. Much of this has been in connection with news of topical disasters – sexual abuse and other concerns. This has no doubt conveyed the idea that counselling is something associated only with alarming crises, but there are far wider applications of counselling than these. Another, less-favourable impression of counselling and psychotherapy sometimes conveyed by the media is that it is a largely self-indulgent, time-consuming pursuit profiting only therapists and those who can afford the luxury of such indulgences. Jokes abound, for example, about the comedian Woody Allen and his alleged 25 years in psycho-analysis.

It is not surprising, given such media caricatures, that people may have confused views about counselling and psychotherapy. Things are not exactly helped, either, by the fact that within and across the professions of counselling and psychotherapy there are different views on what it is all about. There are differently trained practitioners, and a great deal of confusing technical language. Whether you are in acute distress, or you just have a tentative interest in the subject, you are entitled to ask people what is meant by the variety of terms being used. Below we give some brief explanations of some of the key terms, which will be developed throughout the book.

Counselling

Counselling, or to counsel, originally meant advice and advice-giving. But language evolves, and the term now means something quite different from this.

One of the main pioneers of counselling, Carl Rogers developed an approach to helping people in the 1940s known as 'non-directive counselling'. It was given that name because Rogers believed people were not helped effectively by being told by others what to do or think, but benefited more from being helped to trust themselves and find their own solutions. The counsellor's task, according to this view, is to encourage people to take themselves and their own views and feelings seriously until they feel strong enough to do so without the assistance of a counsellor. Counsellors help their clients to achieve this by consistently encouraging them to discover their own inner resources, and to overcome obstacles to living more satisfyingly. Due to Rogers' great influence in the US and the UK, for many people counselling is now considered to be synonymous with a non-directive approach, although there are in fact many others.

Counselling can be considered an enabling, empowering relationship with a disciplined helper. Counsellors are trained to listen to their clients without the interference of their own preoccupations. They are especially concerned to understand as accurately as possible what you are saying, feeling, and thinking. Counselling is not like an everyday social conversation, but rather a focused exploration of particular concerns in a confidential setting, conducted according to clear ethical guidelines. It is often conversational in character, but may sometimes be more emotionally charged than other kinds of conversation. Counselling is always conducted within clear agreements regarding appointment times, time limits, confidentiality, and other boundaries. The subject of counselling may include almost any life dilemma or concern, any personal crisis or continuing worry or aspiration.

As we shall see later, many counsellors do not work in an exclusively non-directive manner, and may in fact use certain specific techniques. Also, while some counsellors may concentrate on short-term crises, others engage in long-term counselling, which aims to help you to understand and change effectively many areas of your functioning. Counselling is always conducted with respect for the self-determination of the client.

Psychotherapy

All that has been said about counselling above also can be said of psychotherapy. Psychotherapy is also 'talking treatment', based on a disciplined relationship between a therapist and client meeting in a confidential setting, and examining personal concerns. Many counsellors are trained as psychotherapists and vice-versa; therapists often say that they practise psychotherapy *and* counselling. So what *is* the difference?

The term 'psychotherapy' originated from Freudian psychoanalysis, and has been in use for about 100 years. Practitioners who have studied and work according to the views of Freud and his followers often refer to themselves as 'psychoanalytically oriented' psychotherapists. Some practitioners insist that the only proper use of the term 'psychotherapy' is in relation to its Freudian origins.

The picture is complicated when you learn, for example, that Carl Rogers referred to his technique both as 'client-centred counselling' and as 'client-centred psychotherapy', and subsequently as 'person-centred counselling/psychotherapy'. In other words, he made no distinction between the two activities. However, people trained according to psychoanalytic principles point out that the work of Rogers and his followers is based on quite different concepts from their own, and cannot legitimately be known as psychotherapy.

The picture is even more complicated when you learn that practitioners following the views of the founders of behavioural, cognitive, Gestalt and other therapeutic schools also call their work psychotherapy (we examine these different approaches in Chapter 6). And then, certain forms of psychological help based on only one, two or three sessions are known as 'brief psychotherapy' – thus dispelling the notion that psychotherapy is distinguished from counselling by its greater length of treatment.

Training for the psychoanalytic psychotherapist usually demands a period of three or more years of part-time immersion in theory and practice. In addition, trainees, as they are called, are required to undertake their own personal therapy in order to examine and understand the intricacies of their inner lives, their motives in wanting to become psychotherapists, and their limitations, problems, and special characteristics. Because this form of therapy and training is based largely on the concept of the unconscious, it is important that trainees become familiar with the vicissitudes of their own unconsciouses.

Once they become qualified psychotherapists, they often spend a long time – sometimes years – with each of their clients, aiming to understand the subtle ways in which their clients' unconscious motives and drives express themselves within the therapy sessions. This kind of psychotherapy, then, usually involves intense scrutiny of the client's utterances, silences, glances, jokes, and other signs of the unconscious expression of deep-seated conflicts.

A central belief in the practice of psychoanalytic psycho-therapy is that the problems or crises which the client brings to therapy are understood to be symptoms of deeper underlying problems, which have to be uncovered in the course of months and years of painstaking analysis.

Counselling vs psychotherapy

Psychotherapy has emerged largely in the context of private practice, where clients pay for their own therapy. It is usually a long-term commitment for which the person frequently must pay a great deal in time and money. Although it is available for free within the NHS, there are often long waiting-lists – sometimes years.

Counselling has emerged in the context of voluntary

organizations and in pastoral and academic settings. It has often been offered as a helping response to specific problems such as marital breakdown, depression, loneliness, bereavement, and so on. Counselling usually involves a once-weekly meeting, while psychotherapy traditionally involves one, two, or more sessions weekly.

Counsellors are sometimes criticized for dealing only with crises while ignoring underlying problems; some say it is an amateur business, conducted by barely trained and un-analysed practitioners. Conversely, psychotherapists may be criticized for claiming to know their clients' minds better than the clients know them themselves, and for encouraging clients to be passive conversationalists instead of active participants in changing their own lives.

There is no way of disguising the fact that counsellors, psychotherapists, and others in the helping and healing business often fail to see eye to eye. The problem faced by you as a potential consumer is what sense to make of these disputes before deciding in whose hands you will place your confidences and your money.

Historically – and one might say accidentally – counselling and psychotherapy have developed as separate activities. Psychotherapy in the UK is now subject to quality control by the United Kingdom Council for Psychotherapy (UKCP) and the British Confederation of Psychotherapists (BCP). Counselling is similarly overseen by the British Association for Counselling (BAC).

Training institutes belonging to the UKCP and BCP are affiliated with various therapeutic traditions (psychoanalytic, humanistic, integrative, and so on). These by no means agree with each other. There is however, a high level of concern for standards and qualifications in the interest of protecting the public.

One major difference between counselling and psychotherapy is that certificates and diplomas in counselling can sometimes be gained within a few months of training, and may not require that trainees have personal therapy whereas it is not possible to complete a psychotherapy training in less than three years and without lengthy personal therapy for the trainee. Having said that, many counselling courses are two or three years long, and many counsellors call themselves either counsellors *or* therapists.

Indeed, as we have seen, in the tradition of client-centred or person-centred counselling/psychotherapy, the terms are considered interchangeable. The closeness of the relationship is demonstrated in the fact that at several annual general meetings of the BAC it has been proposed that the name be changed to incorporate 'psychotherapy'.

This discussion may not make matters clearer in practical terms if you are trying to make the important decision of whether to go to a counsellor or psychotherapist. These points need to be made, however, because there are plenty of myths and misconceptions about the subject. You will not necessarily get better or more professional treatment from a psychotherapist, which is one of the myths put about. Simply put, different people require different kinds of help: you may wish, for example, to discuss an isolated problem briefly or you may want to look at your entire life. Some would say that you look for a counsellor for help in the first case, and for a psychotherapist in the second case. We believe it is not this simple at all. Furthermore, it is still legally defensible for anyone in Britain to call themselves either a counsellor or a psychotherapist, whether they are trained or not. There is at this time such a wide variety of trainings and qualifications in the field, that it is virtually impossible for most people to know the differences in quality.

Some myths and misconceptions

We have drawn attention to the distorted image of counselling that is sometimes portrayed by the media. It would not be surprising if you had a picture of a counsellor as a pleasant but bumbling, well-meaning person offering tea and sympathy, or a person wearing casual clothes and sandals who sits in silence or simply nods and says 'Uh-huh' occasionally. You may picture therapists as bearded men who smoke a pipe and peer at you through their glasses, read your mind, and make secret notes about your underlying problems. Perhaps you have heard scare stories about therapists brainwashing their clients, using some subtle form of hypnosis to extract vast sums of money from them. Such stories are at best caricatures, but most commonly they are complete travesties. Although we have met one or two therapists and counsellors we might describe as a little eccentric, the majority are full of common sense and integrity.

It is because there is so much room for misunderstanding and, in the extreme, abuse of vulnerable people, that we emphasize throughout this book the need to be an informed consumer. For example, it is not uncommon for clients to arrive for a first appointment believing that the counsellor or therapist will know exactly what course of action should be taken. Alternatively, they may believe that the counsellor or therapist will never venture an opinion or statement of their own.

The idea that counselling and psychotherapy are founded on mysterious processes which can only be understood by the highly trained professional perpetuates misunderstandings. Some therapists believe that therapy can only be *experienced* and that any attempt to pre-empt the actual experience is unhelpful and is to intellectualize and defend against it.

There is also the idea that psychotherapy offers to restructure your personality completely; in our experience, it is extremely rare to find any evidence that this has happened. Certainly people may be helped a great deal, and may sometimes say that 'therapy changed my life', but this is not the same as becoming a completely new person which some have fallen prey to.

Counselling is not about passing time and easing loneliness, however, sometimes it is perceived as an opportunity to overcome loneliness or to see someone just for a chat. An appointment at three o'clock every Wednesday may well brighten your life if you live alone, have few or no friends, and no job. But counselling is understood by its practitioners as something other than socializing or chatting. Counsellors may well agree, however, to spend time helping you to look at why you are alone, what opportunities may be available for making friends, and how you can overcome shyness.

Other types of help

Psychoanalysis

Psychoanalysis is the form of treatment pioneered by Freud and developed by others, which places emphasis on inner conflicts, unconscious drives, and the tendency for these to manifest themselves in many subtle ways within the therapeutic relationship. It may be considered a distinct kind of psychotherapy. The patient usually lies on a couch with the analyst seated behind them. The patient then talks about anything that comes into his or her mind, whether recollections of dreams, memories, associations between words, jokes, feelings about the analyst, or whatever. You would attend four or five 50-minute sessions each week, probably for several years. Your analyst's job would be to interpret what you say in order to help you gain insight into how your unconscious is affecting your current life and difficulties.

Psychoanalysts are sometimes, but not always, medically trained, usually as psychiatrists. In the US this is a requirement of the profession, in the UK it is not. In the UK, psychoanalysts train for five or more years. They always have substantial analysis of their own in the training period. They mostly work in private practice. Because psychoanalysis is so very time-consuming, it is rarely available except on a fee-paying basis. (The exception is if you agree to act as a training patient for a supervised trainee.) Patients must expect to commit themselves to a lengthy process and to delayed results. People who have suffered a great deal from early childhood and have complex psychological problems may benefit particularly from psychoanalysis. Unfortunately, one of the paradoxes of psychoanalysis is that some of those perhaps most in need of its gradual, intensive methods are the least able to afford it. Psychoanalysis is also hardly available beyond London and perhaps one or two other very large cities. Although it is one of the approaches least like counselling, we know of one client who, having had years of psychoanalysis, subsequently went to a counsellor, only to remark after some time that it was just like psychoanalysis.

Psychiatry
Psychiatrists are medically trained and then specialize in psychiatry which is the study of mental disorders and the practice of treating them. Psychiatrists are found mainly in hospitals and clinics. They are more likely than counsellors or therapists to have referred to them people who are seriously mentally ill, alcoholic, drug-addicted, and so on. In the UK, psychiatrists have the power to detain (or 'section') people under the Mental Health Act (1983) when they appear to be a danger to themselves or to others.

Psychiatrists do formal assessments on people, asking a series of questions to determine whether they are, for example, experiencing hallucinations, in touch with reality, and able to manage their own life. Suicide risk is usually assessed, as well as previous history of psychiatric disorders, and family history.

Some psychiatrists work privately, and some use psycho-therapeutic methods. Many prescribe particular medications or physical treatments such as electroconvulsive therapy (ECT). Psychiatrists secure for those in need periods of rest, protection, and observation in hospital.

Because psychiatrists working within the NHS are busy and often cannot spend very much time with each individual patient, they may refer them to other services, such as group therapy, occupational therapy, or behaviour therapy. Community psychiatric nurses (CPNs) are psychiatrically trained nurses who visit people in their homes and/or work from community centres, administering and monitoring medications, and in some cases offering counselling.

Because of their medical and psychiatric training, psychiatrists are likely to use terminology relating to mental illness, and to diagnose people by using terms such as manic-depressive, paranoid-schizophrenic, obsessive-compulsive, and so on.

Sometimes people are eligible through private health insurance schemes for psychological treatment provided or endorsed by psychiatrists working privately. For example, if you are suffering from post-traumatic stress disorder, a health insurance pro-gramme is unlikely to pay for you to receive counselling from a counsellor who is not medically trained, and most are not, but may readily pay for similar counselling from a psychiatrist. The exception is where a psychiatrist is able to make a strong case for such a counsellor to be retained.

Some psychiatrists specialize in certain problems, for example anxiety attacks, anorexia nervosa, and addictions. They may be well worth seeking out for their special expertise. Many counsellors are, however, wary of the psychiatric ethos, which has traditionally retained power over people rather than empowering them. There has been a good deal of criticism in recent years of psychiatrists' use of drugs instead of referring people for therapy or counselling. Most counsellors and psychotherapists will have had some exposure to psychiatric medicine within their training. In an extreme emergency, when someone loses control of their normal mental or emotional functioning, they are likely to be referred to their GP and/or a psychiatrist. In some cases counsellors and therapists liaise with psychiatrists in connection with clients who have had psychological breakdowns in the course of their therapy.

There are a few therapeutic residential facilities staffed by therapists who aim to support people going through acute crises without resorting to the usual psychiatric regimes and practices, such as drugs or ECT.

Clinical psychology

All psychologists will have gained at least a first degree in psychology. Clinical psychologists are people who have gone on to gain further qualifications and experience in the field, using psychology in hospital, clinic, and community settings. Clinical psychologists are likely to have seen large numbers of patients, and to have gained considerable experience of a wide range of problems. Traditionally many clinical psychologists have studied behaviour therapy and cognitive therapy. Increasingly they are incorporating into their training and practice principles of person-centred, personal construct, and psychodynamic counselling.

The body which presides over qualifications and standards and oversees the work of clinical psychologists is the British Psychological Society (BPS). Chartered Clinical Psychologists have met certain criteria and are entitled to advertise and practise as such. Clinical psychologists' availability varies from region to region. Whether or not you are referred to one depends on availability, as well as your GP's opinion of and relationship with them. If you have a fairly specific problem, for example, an eating disorder, problem drinking, or agoraphobia, it is worth asking your GP about a possible referral to a clinical psychologist, both because they may have special expertise in your problem, and because their service will be free of charge.

Counselling psychology

A recent development is the establishment of the category of Chartered Counselling Psychologist of the British Psychological Society. This refers to counsellors who have at least a first degree in psychology, plus further training and experience up to a certain standard. There is a debate about the usefulness of the study of psychology to counselling. Some consider that a practitioner who has studied psychology may be better able to understand personality types, may have superior knowledge of certain psychiatric categories, and so on. Others argue that effective counselling need not have a particular grounding in psychology, and may even be impeded by a tendency to interpret behaviour according to psychological tests and criteria. In some NHS settings, counselling psychologists may be employed alongside or instead of clinical psychologists.

Social work

Social workers perform a variety of tasks relating to children; people who are at risk due to mental illness, physical illness or frailty; women who are battered, and families experiencing extreme stress.

Part of social work training often includes the study of Freudian and other theories of human development and problems. Many social workers have had special training in person-centred, psychodynamic, or task-oriented counselling. Probation officers' training is largely identical with that of social workers.

It is sometimes debated whether the help offered by social workers and probation officers can be considered counselling or psychotherapy. It is clear in the minds of many of the practitioners, however, that they are competent and willing to offer this sort of help whenever possible. The existence of the Group for the Advancement of Psychodynamics and Psychotherapy in Social Work (GAPS) testifies to the seriousness with which social workers take the psychotherapeutic aspect of their work.

Co-counselling

Co-counselling is a form of reciprocal counselling or therapy. It is learned in classes, and then practised by people by agreement, without payment. In pairs, one person agrees first to counsel his or her partner, and then the other person counsels the first. Some people prefer this method of counselling because it is egalitarian.

Critics of co-counselling suggest that it is insufficient to help deep-seated problems, and that it cannot help anyone in need of the one-way, expert help available only from trained therapists. Co-counselling should not be passed over as a possible form of help, however. You may wish to find or set up such an arrangement for example if you live in a fairly remote area where there are no counsellors. Certain books are available which set out to teach the rudiments of co-counselling.

Befriending

If friends were able to help us with our personal problems, there might be no need for counsellors and therapists. For a variety of reasons, friends are often not enough. But what about befriending?

Agencies such as the Samaritans regard their work as primarily telephone befriending, or listening, rather than as counselling or therapy. The Samaritans stems from a pastoral background and regards itself as a humanitarian venture aimed at preventing suicide and at offering some degree of companionship in an alienating society.

Befriending is also carried out by people working in community care, with people who have serious mental health problems, AIDS and other isolating conditions. Befrienders are also sometimes known as 'buddies'; they may arrange to visit people at home, accompany them on trips, help them with chores, or simply spend time with them, easing their loneliness.

Self-help

There are many varieties of self-help: self-analysis, bibliotherapy, journal keeping, co-counselling, support groups, mutual-aid organizations, and so on. What they all have in common is the attempt to remedy a problem or problems without necessarily resorting to professional help.

Freud recognized that some progress could be made with one's own problems by analysing one's dreams, daydreams, thoughts, and feelings. Psychoanalysts in general, however, regard self-analysis as insufficient in itself. In recent years many self-help books have appeared, which seek to help people solve their own problems. Interactive workbooks, for example, encourage you to complete certain exercises; audiotapes aim to help you to relax or become more assertive; and various methods of journal keeping seek to encourage self-reflection. Such methods are well worth a 'first try' for anyone who is troubled, or who simply wishes to gain a new perspective on his or her life.

Since psychotherapy has existed only for 100 years, people must have had ways of coping before that time – self-reliance, support from neighbours and extended families, and succour and guidance from religion and priests. Alcoholics Anonymous is an outstanding example of a mutual-aid organization without professionals, which relies on the experiences of 'fellow recovering alcoholics'. Such people know about the stubbornness of drink problems, and are committed to helping each other.

There are similar self-help groups which attack the problems of compulsive eating, shopping, and other forms of addictive behaviour. Some of the people in these groups know from personal experience what the problem is like, and often extend a great deal of help to others. There are also many smaller support groups that have been established for specific concerns, for example, ME, or single parenthood. It is also possible to begin your own self-help group.

Advice and guidance
There may be times when you want firm advice. For example, if you have a serious medical condition, you might ask your doctor what she or he considers best for you, based on their experience. If he or she begins to 'counsel' you at this point, refusing to answer your questions directly, you might well become frustrated. There is, then, a place for advice and guidance, and it is best to be clear about when you need it – and who can give it.

There are services which give information on marriage from the perspective of tax, immigration, religious affiliation, and so on. There is no reason why you should not consult professionals in these fields, but you need to be clear who such professionals are. You would be disappointed if you approached a marital guidance organization such as Relate for information on the material advantages and disadvantages of marriage. The counselling available at Relate has to do with the emotional relationship between couples, rather than with anything in the legal and financial sphere. Some couples have been disappointed when their counsellor did not give them practical advice on improving their marriage, but instead concentrated on their psychological problems.

If you were questioning whether or not to have an abortion, you might wish to talk about your ethical and religious beliefs, and to ask practical medical questions. You might get the information you need from books, or from your doctor, or a specialist service. You might then discuss your feelings with friends. If you were in a crisis that signified yet another thing going wrong in your life, you might want to talk about this pattern of unhappiness with a counsellor or psychotherapist.

Counsellors in family planning clinics would probably have the kind of information you need to make your decision, but even they would not direct you one way or the other: the ethos of counselling is based on respect for your autonomy, your ability and right to know your own feelings, and to make your own decisions.

We hope the above examples of psychological help, and the places and people offering it will help to guide you towards a decision. However, don't assume that the moment you run into a problem you need counselling. Often we experience problems about which we can do nothing; we just have to endure them until they pass. There is an argument that we should consider the merits of self-determination, self-reliance, and hard work in overcoming our problems. Weigh up for yourself the merits of such arguments, and consider the guidelines in the following chapters about the merits of professional therapy; only *you* can make the final choice and decision about what is best suited to your needs.

2
Who Can Benefit?

The short answer to this question is that almost anyone can benefit from counselling and psychotherapy. Exactly *how much* and in *what ways* is more difficult to answer.

There is a large group of common problems brought to counsellors which have a good prospect of being resolved. These include some forms of depression, anxiety, bereavement, identity crises, and relationship problems. These may be contrasted with another, less hopeful group, which includes stubborn addictions, serious mental health problems or mental illness, and physical or psychosomatic illnesses. One way of illustrating the scope of counselling and therapy is to look at several examples of conditions less likely to be helped.

Who cannot benefit

Serious mental health problems

For someone diagnosed as schizophrenic, there is little hope that talking therapies will have much impact, although there are a few practitioners who believe long-term therapy can help. It is now widely accepted, however, that the best way of managing – but not curing – schizophrenia is through medication, mainly by what are known as the major tranquillizers.

People who are diagnosed as schizophrenic and who live lives that are intermittently miserable but tolerable naturally wish for a breakthrough. Counselling, especially that provided free in some mental health agencies, is at times grasped as a possible panacea. We have known counsellors who have made valiant attempts to help schizophrenic clients to change fundamentally. While often it is possible to achieve a great deal of understanding of the factors that may have led to mental illness, talking on its own has little chance of ending the person's misery. It is possible, however, to help someone with schizophrenia to manage their lives better. The key is acceptance. If the client is hoping against hope that their illness can be totally transformed, then counselling or therapy is likely to fail. If, however, the client is saying, 'I know I may be like this forever, but I still want to get on with my life. I want to form relationships and to work,' then there is hope for a modestly positive outcome. They may then, for example, be helped to practise social skills which will help them to explain their condition to others. He or she may be helped to commit to a regimen of medication, diet, exercise, and healthy lifestyle, which will stand them in better stead for getting work and making relationships.

An important word of warning: it is possible that schizophrenic conditions can be made worse in the short term by therapy which unwisely, and perhaps aggressively, attempts to uncover hidden causes and conflicts. Working with schizophrenia is a special skill, and requires special guidance and supervision as well as knowledge of medication. It is also important for counsellors and therapists to liaise closely with a person's doctor or psychiatrist.

There are other mental health problems which, although not as unyielding as schizophrenia, are cause for particular concern. Severe or clinical depression will probably not benefit from psychotherapy alone. A course of appropriate medication may be needed before or during the therapy.

Anyone who has serious sleep difficulties, loss of appetite, lethargy, feelings of extreme hopelessness, and frequent thoughts of suicide needs more attention than can be given by most counsellors or psychotherapists. A medical, probably psychiatric, assessment should be considered in such cases. It would be unethical for counsellors to attempt to work with anyone so seriously depressed without consulting other professionals.

In any case where a person's behaviour is dangerously unpredictable or life-threatening (theirs or someone else's), additional help is required. If you or someone you know exhibits extremes of self-harming behaviour, or is even slightly delusional (hearing voices, for example), on no account is counselling or psychotherapy enough in its own right to contain the problem. Medical or psychiatric help is needed.

Physical illness

A similar case can be made for people suffering from cancer, AIDS or other life-threatening or terminal illnesses. In our view, counselling and psychotherapy are unlikely to cure or even affect such illnesses. There have been claims that certain methods of counselling have led to remission of symptoms. Positive thinking is sometimes considered to have the power to alter the course of a malignancy, for example. We cannot deny that this is a possibility, but it is certainly not an everyday occurrence, and we believe there are probably more cases of disappointment relating to such hopes than there are cases of successful treatment. Counselling can help people come to terms with, for example, cancer, by helping them to define themselves in terms other than their illness. It can help them to keep their illness in proportion, instead of making themselves even more upset and ill than they need be. Counselling may even help them to get a great deal from a shortened life. It may sometimes simply provide relief through the expression of grief, anger and perhaps, finally, acceptance.

There is a school of thought that asserts that suppressed anger, for example, can lead to illness; we have even heard the assertion that denied anger causes cancer. There are examples of illness and some research that can be naively interpreted in this way. For people who believe such ideas, they may enter into particular kinds of therapy which promise to increase their ability to express anger, and thus to avoid getting cancer.

In our view, serious physical illnesses are properly the domain of medical practitioners, whether conventional or complementary. You are advised to think carefully about any hopes of avoiding or eliminating cancer through counselling or psychotherapy. It is of course delightful if in the course of your therapy your physical illnesses disappear or improve – but there can be no guarantee of such results. *Above all, you should on no account abandon medical help in favour of purely psychological help in such circumstances.*

Psychosomatic illness

'Psychosomatic' means a psychologically induced physical symptom or illness. Within the psychosomatic domain, there are many questions about whether counselling or therapy can ameliorate or cure certain conditions. People are turning to counsellors for help with their stress reactions, for example, which may sometimes include raised blood pressure, sleep disorder, dizziness, nausea, and other disturbances. Counselling often does help to lessen the effects of stress, or can help a person to find ways of changing their attitudes and lifestyle. But if you work in a setting where impossibly high expectations are set for you, all the work you do in counselling may be invalidated by the realities of stress within your company.

The possibility also exists, unfortunately, for misdiagnosis. People are sometimes told they are suffering from stress and anxiety symptoms and that they should consult a counsellor when in fact they have an organic problem. Neither counsellors nor psychotherapists are likely to have a great deal of medical knowledge, and naturally proceed on the assumption that emotional and psychological factors are uppermost. Neurological and thyroid problems, for example, sometimes manifest as anxiety symptoms, and the unwary counsellor or therapist can proceed with the best of intentions to treat them psychologically. As well as wasting time and money, this can mean a dangerous delay in getting correct medical treatment. If you suffer the symptoms of severe depression, post-traumatic stress disorder and other such significant mood-altering conditions, you may need to take certain prescribed drugs at the same time as being in therapy.

In the case of premenstrual tension, although there is considerable debate among psychologists about whether it actually exists, there are many women willing to seek both medical and psychotherapeutic help. This is an area about which not enough is currently known, and shows how you should take into account the lack of knowledge when contemplating counselling.

Addictions

Another category of difficult problems is the addictions. There are special reasons for not investing too much hope in the potency of counselling or therapy in this area. Drug and alcohol addiction are particularly stubborn conditions, both psychologically and physically. Many drugs have addictive properties, which means that all the talking and understanding in the world probably will not be able to overthrow them.

Added to this is the observation that addicts of all types are frequently deceptive – deceiving both themselves and others about how committed they are to change, and how well they are doing. Frequently addicts need residential treatment, tough, confrontational regimes, help from fellow sufferers, as well as medical assistance if they are to have any realistic chance of getting better. At a certain stage of recovery they may well benefit from individual counselling, but even then the possibilities of relapse are high. One residential centre we know of reports that its typical new client has already tried and failed with at least four or five previous therapists. Such people need to be clear that counselling is not magic and cannot work against their addiction without hard work and genuine commitment.

Lack of commitment

You may have a problem that is not as severe as these, and which may well benefit from counselling – yet you yourself may not be convinced that you are in need of help.

Let us suppose that all your friends and family are worried about how depressed you seem, and they urge you to seek counselling. You get as far as making an appointment and arriving for a first session, but you are nevertheless unconvinced that you have a serious problem, or that counselling can help you. Really, you have agreed to keep the appointment just to pacify everyone around you.

Counselling can be very successful with depression, but it cannot work in spite of the person – there has to be co-operation. This is well known to counsellors. People sometimes arrive having been sent by partners or managers, or perhaps by GPs, all of whom of course mean well. But if you are half-hearted, or even utterly uncommitted to giving counselling a decent chance, it is unlikely to work. Paul went for counselling and reported to the counsellor that he had come to save his marriage. After one or two sessions it became obvious to his counsellor that he had come because his wife had given him an ultimatum. He himself had no serious intention of reflecting on or changing his behaviour.

There are people who have experienced deep disappointments in life, sometimes from a very early age. Some seem to make a career out of proving that everyone lets them down or fails them. In therapy such people often make their way from one therapist to another with the unconscious or half-conscious intention of getting the therapist to fail – to repeat over and over again the initial disappointment. It is quite a different matter if you are in genuine distress but somewhat wary of counselling or unsure if it is what you need; at least then you may give it a good chance to succeed.

Who can benefit?

Crises

Many people who are driven by a crisis to seek help and who secure it reasonably quickly are helped by counselling. When something happens in our life which shakes us up and challenges the apparent security of our everyday routines and our self-image, we experience a kind of doubt and pain which can be very motivating. As the well-known saying goes, crisis is opportunity. We are not saying that crises are a wonderful thing, but any major change of circumstances forces us to reconsider our basic values, and can potentially lead to new and enriching experiences. If your partner leaves you, you are made redundant, your mother dies, or you reach the age of 50 without achieving what you had set your heart on, you are likely to experience stress. You may feel a little sad and demoralized temporarily, or you may begin to experience acute distress and panic. The humdrum world with which you were so familiar has suddenly changed and become insecure.

Responses to a crisis vary from flight and denial (you may get drunk or pretend to yourself that you do not feel so bad); to breakdown (you may become seriously depressed, isolated, and suicidal). It is at the point where you feel acute distress but retain enough control and hope, and self-respect, that you may reach out for help.

Although people who contact counsellors at this stage are highly motivated in the sense that they wish to ease the pain and keep some control over their lives, often, as soon as the immediate distress lessens, or circumstances improve slightly, the counselling is abandoned. No doubt we may fear that if we let ourselves dwell on our distress by discussing it in therapy we may temporarily feel worse, or that we may discover truths about ourselves we would rather not know. This is a pivotal point. Some psychotherapists feel that entering therapy is an important and deliberate choice, not a matter of reaching for immediate relief from a painful crisis; you are more likely to benefit in the long run, this argument goes, if you commit yourself to a lengthy and difficult process of self-examination. On the other hand, people can derive a great deal from a relatively short period of therapeutic counselling. The benefits of what are known as single-session therapy and time-limited therapy are in part due to the critical timing of the help given, and the heightened motivation brought by clients in distress.

Some people benefit from remaining in counselling after the phase of symptomatic relief has passed. When you no longer feel acutely distressed about your redundancy or relationship break-down, you may sense that there are deeper issues underlying your crisis, and you may wish to explore these. For example, if you believe the end of a relationship was nothing more than bad luck, you may look forward to better luck next time, but if you suspect that something in your attitude led to the relationship ending, and is likely to lead to future difficulties, you may decide to take a good long look at yourself in counselling or therapy.

Sometimes it is helpful to explore adverse childhood experiences and to uncover the attitudes we have carried forward from them in order to learn that we no longer need to repeat past patterns of behaviour. In this sense a crisis is telling us that all is not well inside us, it is saying that major internal 'repairs' are called for. On the other hand, a crisis resulting in a panic attack may lead to nothing more than satisfactorily finding ways in counselling to overcome the panic attacks. In other words, there is no absolute rule about what any individual should want from therapy.

Readiness

You may decide quite rationally, without pressure from a crisis, to begin counselling or therapy. You find, however, that after two years little is happening, and you terminate the counselling or therapy. Some years later, in a dilemma about your direction in life, you again seek help. This time, however, you find the therapy or counselling a much more rewarding experience. It may be that you were too young and too uninvolved in relationships before, or that now you feel sufficiently mature to take full advantage of the reflective nature of therapy. Whatever the explanation, it is a fact that some people have several experiences of therapy or counselling, yet feel more ready for and helped by it at some stages than at others, or they may learn from one experience what is unhelpful for them, and subsequently search for a kind of therapy that is more beneficial. The most effective way of learning what is right for you may be through trial and error.

Another explanation for readiness is that things have to fall into place mentally for us. Perhaps we simply have to experience certain things in life, to exhaust certain hopes and dreams, before

deciding that we are ready for the kind of self-confrontation that therapy involves. There is also the view that there are times in life when we are more likely to seek help, perhaps in adolescence, at about age 30, in midlife, and so on.

Motivation

If you are highly motivated to do something about yourself, you stand a better chance of succeeding than if you are half-hearted. If you have read about counselling, you believe in it, and you feel a strong need to change, you are more likely to benefit than someone who has only a vague sense of what counselling is, is unsure whether they have any problems, and is not committed.

Sometimes personality and other factors are significant. One of the paradoxes of counselling is that perhaps those people who already have the most in the sense of material success are the ones who benefit most. Those who are most depressed, however, are among those least likely to be able to motivate themselves, since depression is often characterized by hopelessness. There may be a zone of optimal motivation lying midway between the hopelessness of serious depression and the complacency of an easy life. In order to benefit from counselling, the person is presumably in some degree of distress, uncertainty or dissatisfaction, but not so much that he or she is incapacitated, or so little that they will have no commitment. It is sometimes said that a degree of hardship is a motivating factor: if you have to give up certain things in order to be able to afford therapy, perhaps you will value it more. If you have plenty of money and can just as easily afford to take a holiday as pay for therapy, you may be tempted to take the easier option.

Psychological-mindedness

This term simply means that you are disposed to analyse matters in a psychological light. It does not mean that you are an avid consumer of books on psychology, or that you have studied psychology at all. It refers to an interest in understanding everyday events in relation to thoughts and feelings: you wonder why John reacted the way he did when you spoke to him – you do not assume it was something he ate, or that it was due to the stars, or the present socio-economic climate. You question whether you upset him, or whether he had had a row with his partner. To attempt to understand the behaviour of others or oneself in such terms is to be psychologically-minded. If when I feel rather low I automatically reach for tablets, blame the government, or my genetic inheritance, I am not demonstrating psychological-mindedness.

Psychological-mindedness, then, implies a particular orientation in one's thinking. If you are willing to consider events in terms of how they are created or interpreted by people, and if you are willing to take responsibility for your own actions, you are likely to benefit from counselling or therapy. If you cannot see connections between behaviour patterns and possible explanations for these, you may have difficulty. Psychological-mindedness implies an interest in what makes you tick, and an assumption that you are individually responsible to some extent for what happens in your life. It also implies that you have a certain amount of power to affect circumstances.

Class and Culture

Counselling and psychotherapy, although not necessarily rooted within the subject of psychology, are based on various analyses of individuals' thoughts, feelings, and behaviour. Therapists are concerned primarily with individual human development, with what goes wrong in people's minds and how it may be corrected by new understanding. They are not primarily politicians, sociologists, pharmacologists, or ecologists, for example. Most therapists accept that there are real social problems which impinge on us, but their focus is on how you can be helped within your present circumstances, or how you might change your circumstances after you have understood more about yourself.

It has been noted that prime candidates for therapy are those who fall within the YAVIS category: Young, Attractive, Verbal, Intelligent, Successful. For example, Paul has a good job and is highly paid and valued as a colleague and friend. Lately, however, he has wondered about his wife and family – whether they need or appreciate him. He wonders if he should seek professional help. Rita, on the other hand, is a single parent living on a council estate, on a low income. She has few friends and no holidays. Lately she has been feeling extremely depressed, and sometimes hits her young son in sheer frustration. Clearly, Paul and Rita are in very different circumstances. Paul can decide to find a therapist or counsellor tomorrow, should he choose. For Rita, every day is a battle against penury and depression. Her very surroundings reinforce the message that she is not highly valued by society.

You may not resemble Paul or Rita, but you can learn something from them. You may benefit from therapy if you need it and can get it, but if you need it and have little or no access to such services, then the question of it benefiting you is academic. Added to this is whether your circumstances are so adverse that any amount of talking or psychological insight could compensate for them or change them. As for Rita, if your everyday experience of life is extremely tough, you have a great deal to struggle with on top of inner conflicts: finding someone to babysit for you while you get a bus to your nearest community mental health centre and back is an extra struggle.

Having said this, we have all heard the adage that the rich may be just as miserable as the poor. Even in the most terrible circumstances, some people may fall apart psychologically, and some survive reasonably well. What this suggests is that individual differences help some people to survive, and even flourish, in almost any conditions.

The idea that there is always hope, no matter what the circumstances, is central to counselling and therapy; the idea that small, positive steps are better than no steps at all is also central. If you live in highly adverse circumstances, counselling will not transport you from housing estate to a leafy suburb, but it could help you to survive a little better.

Women, black people, homosexuals, people with disabilities, and other minority groups have long complained that not only are their particular needs ignored, but they are treated by others, and particularly by those in powerful positions, as second-class citizens. If you belong to one or more of these groups, your daily reality may be that society devalues or demeans you. If you cannot secure employment because you are black or disabled, for example, no amount of counselling will conjure up a job for you. In such cases, you should realize that counselling alone may not help you to get what you need, and that certain kinds of counselling or counsellor may benefit you more than others.

Psychotherapy has been criticized as being unduly white and Western in its assumptions. The belief that we are all autonomous, for example, seems unquestionable to many of us, but would be objected to by those observing certain religious and cultural traditions which emphasize the authority of God, priests, and family leaders. Obedience to tradition is anathema to many counsellors, who may espouse a free-thinking, perhaps libertarian, approach to life. 'A woman's right to choose' whether or not to have an abortion is a position likely to be upheld by most British counsellors and therapists, but opposed by many people affiliated with fundamentalist religions. Adherence to traditional family values may be expected among members of certain cultures, yet questioning conventional family values and traditions lies at the heart of much Western psychology and psychotherapy.

If you belong to a culture which is at odds with the predominant one in which you live, you may wish to consider carefully whether you wish your cultural values to be challenged, respected, or upheld.

Psychotherapy and counselling can help a wide variety of people, with a variety of problems, in a variety of circumstances. You can be helped as an individual or as a couple or family. You may even be helped effectively as a working team or organization, since some counsellors and counselling psychologists act as consultants to organizations. There are no guarantees that you will get exactly what you want from therapy, but if you think it might realistically benefit you, there is probably little reason not to try it. There are, however, limits to the effectiveness of this kind of therapy, and you are advised to examine carefully whether your concerns and resources match the kinds of help available.

3
What Can You Expect?

People come to counselling with all sorts of fears and fantasies: 'I hope this person will be able to help me stop having these awful panic attacks,' is a reasonable hope, 'Once I've sorted out my problems, I'll have the world at my feet,' is less realistic and reasonable. Whatever thoughts go through your mind when you contemplate counselling, this sort of hoping and fantasizing is probably an unavoidable process.

Perhaps the more unreasonable, though not uncommon, expectations include the idea that the counsellor will know exactly what is wrong with you and how to fix it, and that once it is fixed you will be completely transformed into a new person. Unfortunately, some therapies pander to this fantasy. You may read or hear about promises of psychological 'rebirth', removal of psychosomatic illnesses, access to sublime states of mind, the development of special powers, and the transcendence of all neurotic symptoms. We believe all such claims to be irresponsible nonsense. There is no harm in wishing to change large parts of your life – but you will not achieve this in psychotherapy or counselling, and you are more likely to be helped modestly than dramatically.

The counsellor or psychotherapist

Counsellors and therapists are ordinary human beings who have chosen to make a living from listening to and discussing people's problems and concerns with them. They do not have superior insights into life, higher moral standards, better physical health, or other fancied attributes. They simply claim to have studied a certain amount of theory concerning human development and behaviour, to have practised therapy for a certain period, and often to have undergone their own personal therapy. This should be kept in proportion. It is all too easy to idealize therapists and counsellors – who, being human, are not necessarily immune to such flattery.

It is thought by many that the personal qualities of the counsellor or therapist and the kind of emotional climate they provide are the most important ingredients of therapy. At the same time, therapists differ in the ways they present themselves, some believing it is more helpful to the client if they are warm and genuine, others believing that a degree of formality or neutrality is beneficial. Some may therefore greet you warmly, and others will seem rather cool, some may shake your hand and engage in small talk, while others will refrain altogether from such social niceties, some may offer you a cup of tea, while others would never consider it. Counsellors' behaviour is not invariably dictated by their theoretical beliefs, however; inevitably the strengths and weaknesses of their own personalities will also affect their behaviour towards you.

The counselling environment

Counsellors' and psychotherapists' consulting rooms also can be very different, ranging from plush to shabby; from an office to a room in their own home, the latter being probably the most common. Whatever and wherever the room is, you should be assured of complete privacy. It should be virtually soundproof, particularly if you are likely to want to cry or shout. On the subject of noise, it is preferable if the telephone does not ring while you are having your counselling session, and your counsellor should certainly not interrupt you to take a call.

Therapists differ in their views about how anonymous or otherwise their room should be. One argument is that if the room is quite bare the client will not be distracted and therefore will be more likely to have to think deeply about their inner life. Other therapists and counsellors may provide a setting with colour, textures, and signs of their own taste. The setting should be welcoming, comfortable, safe, warm, and conducive to intimacy. Usually the counsellor and you will be seated in ordinary chairs. Some therapists provide a couch or bed on which you can lie. Others use floor cushions and other props for the kind of therapy which encourages a great deal of physical self-expression.

You should have access to a toilet within the premises, and, if possible, a waiting-room, or area. Many counsellors are not able to provide waiting-rooms, so you should be prepared to arrive and leave punctually. Awkwardness can be avoided by not asking to use the counsellor's telephone as you are leaving, to arrange for a taxi which then takes 20 minutes to arrive!

Core conditions

There are certain core conditions in counselling which are a reliable guide to what to expect. These are:

- respect or non-judgemental acceptance – sometimes called 'unconditional positive regard'
- genuineness – the counsellor being their own person and not taking on an unreal role, which is also known as congruence
- empathy, whereby the counsellor is able to understand you from your point of view.

Respect

You should be respected, and your concerns taken seriously; on no account should you feel belittled or humiliated, especially when you want to talk about aspects of your behaviour that you feel are unpleasant or undesirable. Expect to be accepted as a struggling, fallible human being like everyone else – including the counsellor!

It is possible that you hold religious, political, or moral views which the counsellor does not share. You would expect to feel free to discuss them without censure, you would certainly not expect any counsellor to attempt to convert you to their own beliefs.

Genuineness

Genuineness is more problematic. Counsellors belonging to the humanistic schools (see Chapter 6) place a high premium on being open and genuine. They believe that by being in touch with their own feelings, by being true to themselves and sharing their honest feelings about you, they will serve you best. This does not mean they will always tell you exactly what they think about you, and it certainly does not mean they will cruelly confront you with what they consider unpleasant about you. Rather, it means they will carefully monitor their own responses to you, will not confuse their own feelings with yours, and will be prepared to challenge you when it seems to be in your best interests.

Other counsellors, particularly of the psychodynamic school, may not express their feelings as directly, so that you are free to imagine and feel what you like about them, with the understanding that such fantasies and feelings usually stem from your past.

The more such counsellors 'withhold' themselves, the purer are your own feelings and thoughts likely to be, and it should prove more beneficial to examine and work with them. This argument is underlined by the idea that you do not enter therapy to strike up a new relationship with the therapist, but to resolve existing problems; therefore the genuineness of the therapist is not an issue. Your own opinions about these matters are important, and Chapter 6 should help you to decide further on such matters.

Empathy

Quite simply, you cannot be helped by someone who cannot understand what you are saying, how you are feeling, and how you look at the world. To have empathy means that the person is able to put aside his or her own preoccupations and assumptions, and strive to hear and see things as you do. He or she does not identify with you exactly, but 'tunes in' to your experiences, concerns, lifestyle, and relationships – as far as is humanly possible, they try to grasp what it must be like to be you.

The counsellor may tell you how he understands your world, your everyday experiences and your particular problems so that he can check if he has understood you correctly. He may occasionally say something that is based on a hunch about how you feel and why you feel that way. Often he will simply be silent as he digests and thinks about what you are saying and what non-verbal clues you give to your state of mind. Silence, although sometimes uncomfortable, is not intended as a clever trick but as a means of understanding you and helping you to see your own way out of your present impasse. All counsellors should be open to being corrected if they have failed to understand you; equally, you should feel able to correct them if they have made a mistake.

Normally, you can expect your therapist to be consistently available for you at appointment times, and not to change or cancel appointments without exceptionally good reason. It is possible that if you are being seen in a very busy clinic your therapist may interrupt the session to deal with something urgent, but this is unusual, as well as discourteous. You would expect, too, that the therapist will be emotionally and physically constant, rather than moody, distractable, or frequently unwell. You may have little choice in certain circumstances other than to put up with less than these expectations, for example, if you depend on a free service, but most counselling organizations, be they statutory, voluntary, or commercial, have channels for consumer feedback and complaints.

The contract

Counselling and psychotherapy, in Britain at least, is not well regulated from a legal perspective. You may expect your therapist to have been properly trained and qualified, but she or he is not legally obliged to have done so (this is dealt with in more detail in Chapter 5). You may expect that if you go to see a therapist to have your panic attacks or cat phobia cured, she or he will cure them. Unfortunately, counselling and therapy are not exact sciences; few, if any, counsellors can guarantee definite results. This is because the current stage of professional development of counselling and therapy does not permit us to predict scientific-ally what will occur in any given case; also, individuals are unique: one person's panic attacks, for example, may not yield to the same treatment as another's.

You should not expect a counsellor or therapist to promise to get rid of your distress; indeed, many feel that no counsellor should ever promise particular results, however optimistic or experienced they may be. Counsellors, however, are by nature optimistic people, and will naturally be encouraging. You should not confuse being offered hope with being given a definitive promise.

Ideally, it is considered good practice for counsellors and therapists to make clear statements, verbally or in writing, about their qualifications, confidentiality, details of fees, availability, cancellation policies, and so on (see Chapter 5). Such a statement forms the basis of your contract, and provides you with certain baselines. If your counsellor seriously contravenes the terms of the contract, if they refuse to negotiate helpfully with you them-selves, you can at least consider complaining to their professional association.

Counsellors will vary greatly in the extent to which they make initial and ongoing contracts. Some prefer clear verbal agreements at the start of every session about what you want from the session, what you intend to do between sessions, and so on. Some will seek your agreement at the beginning of treatment that you will, for example, give up smoking, over-eating, cutting yourself, or suicide attempts, and may refuse to work with you if you do not comply. Others will rarely or never insist on agreements or contracts, regarding everything as part of the therapy. Therapists owe you a duty of care, in other words to act professionally and responsibly, but they cannot be responsible for everything that happens to you. Your part in the negotiations is to be as clear as possible about what you need, and what you are not happy with.

A poorly developed aspect of therapy is the understanding of informed consent, which means your right to be clearly informed about a treatment before receiving it. Counselling and therapy are treatments that involve you intimately, and may have a profound impact on your mental health – you have the right to know what your counsellor intends to do in relation to your problems, how they conceptualize them, what approach they intend to take, and some explanation about their procedures. Unfortunately, in our view, some therapists prefer to retain a certain mystique or authority, and in line with this may refuse to explain what they are doing or why. Now, it is true that you can become obsessive about explanations, and, as we have mentioned, the course of counselling is not necessarily predictable. Do not be afraid, however, of asking your counsellor to tell you why dreams are important, why long silences are helpful, or why it is necessary for you to make specific goals.

Commitment

Entering counselling or psychotherapy is for many people an enormous commitment in terms of money, time, hope, and emotional energy. The extent of that commitment varies according to your needs and wishes: you may consult a counsellor once about some debt-related problems and the stress of dealing with them, or you may enter into a psychoanalysis lasting ten years; you may receive a free service, or you may plough your life savings into therapy; you may visit a counsellor who lives in the next road, or you may go abroad for therapy. The range of commitment is enormous and varied. You need to think carefully about the extent of your therapeutic needs and discuss these openly with your therapist or counsellor. Some of the practicalities are discussed below.

Time

Let us look first at the weekly time commitment. A typical

scenario is as follows: your counsellor asks you to commit yourself to a trial number of one-hour, or fifty-minute sessions, probably at the same time each week; if these proceed satisfactorily, you may be told that counselling or therapy often takes a few months, or perhaps a couple of years, depending on the nature of your problems, how long you have had them, how old you are, and so on.

You will next need to agree on appointment times. If you are working, it may have to be an evening or lunchtime appointment. Depending on your counsellor's location, you will have to travel there and back. Some people find they need a little time after their sessions to be alone to reflect. Your counsellor may ask you to take part in homework exercises related to the counselling, and these will also take time. Rarely does a counselling session take up only a neat hour, so you must plan for this accordingly.

Next is the longer-term commitment. Because therapists work differently, some may expect to see you very briefly – for example, in some agencies you may be limited to three or four free sessions – others may ask you to commit yourself to blocks of sessions, say, six at a time. Or you may be asked to agree to a lengthy process of a year, two years, or more. Some will agree to see you weekly, fortnightly, or even less frequently; others may insist that you attend at least twice a week, and perhaps more often. Remember that you have a right to say no, or to negotiate, or to seek help elsewhere.

If a therapist says she wishes to see you twice a week for at least two years, it is not necessarily a reflection of how disturbed you are or how entrenched your problems are, although it may be. It may reflect the therapist's own preferred way of working, and the therapeutic tradition in which they have trained. Realistically, if you have serious or complex concerns, then the process is likely to take longer. If you have been depressed for several years, for example, your therapy will almost certainly take longer than it would for someone who has recently developed a mild phobia.

It is often not possible for the counsellor to know in advance how long your therapy will take. You may begin modestly, with a few uncommitted sessions, then get a taste for it, and go on to commit yourself for several years. It is not uncommon for people to have several different experiences of therapy scattered across the years: you need not think of therapy as being a once-and-for-all, all-or-nothing commitment. Many therapists, however, do think of it in these terms. So you may need to discuss such expectations very clearly, and you should not be intimidated by therapists who suggest that only total commitment will suffice. (These issues are discussed further in Chapter 9.)

Money

The cost of therapy ranges from nothing to vast amounts. Counselling from a voluntary agency, a student counselling service, a workplace welfare service, or an NHS facility will almost certainly be free of charge, or amount to only minimal donations. On the other hand, if you seek the most prestigious psychotherapy available, you can pay anything in excess of £50 an hour. We have heard figures of £100 or so, for each hourly consultation, but we have no way of discovering who holds the record! According to an article in *The Observer Magazine* (30 Jan., 1994) top sex therapists in the UK can command fees of £150 an hour. High fees like this will probably reflect the higher status profession of the practitioner (e.g., psychiatrists), qualifications, length of experience and reputation, and the setting. It generally follows that if you see therapists in affluent areas, you pay more accordingly. If you seek out prestigious practitioners with Harley Street addresses, for example, you will definitely be paying at the very upper end of the scale.

In Britain, at the time of writing (1994), the *typical* rate for private counselling and psychotherapy is between £15 and £30 per hour (sometimes this means an actual hour, sometimes the so-called '50-minute hour'). Practitioners vary in their charges according to where they live, what their experience and qualifications are, what their overheads are, what they think their services are worth, and what their political and moral views are.

Paying £25 an hour to someone for talking and listening to you may seem exorbitant. Counsellors and therapists, however, usually pay for their own training, which, including personal therapy may cost in total anything from £2,000 to £20,000, or more. They then have to pay for annual professional memberships, accreditation, insurance, continuing supervision, additional training and therapy, specialist journals, consulting room rental, and so on. Time has to be devoted to case-study and supervision. All this behind-the-scenes work is, of course, invisible to the client. Most counsellors and therapists do not see eight clients a day, every day of the week, 52 weeks a year, but devote time to reflection, study, supervision, and other necessarily replenishing tasks. Very few counsellors go into this work to make their fortune; for most, the overall remuneration is fairly modest. It is worth putting therapists' fees in this context so that you understand what you are paying for.

Some counsellors can afford to keep their fees low because they may have another income; many reserve a few places for clients on low incomes, or are willing to negotiate rates on a sliding scale of what your annual income is. Some offer a first free session, whereas others charge more than usual for the first session. Some may charge more for out-of-hours (evening) appointments than for daytime ones. Some will vary your fees according to whether you are employed or not. Trainee or newly qualified counsellors and therapists working under the auspices of a training institute may charge lower rates. Depending on the kind of therapy, you may sometimes book longer sessions, lasting for an hour and a half or two hours, for which you may be charged pro rata or a separate rate. Some therapists fix their rates; others will raise them annually in line with inflation, or other factors.

You may wish or need to calculate how much you are likely to spend in total. Paying £25 for one session a week for about a year will easily amount to £1,000 a year, for example. But you may have to pay even more than this for each session, and attend for several years. You may decide to attend sessions two or three times a week, or more. It is not unknown for people to pay out £75 a week or more for several years.

Some people feel so distressed and unable to cope without regular time with a therapist that they are willing to make sacrifices in other areas of their lives. They may decide that it is more important to go without a car, for example, or expensive clothes. Some calculate that if they cut back or give up their indulgences or bad habits, they will be able to afford therapy. It makes sense that if you are going to devote yourself to achieving greater mental health, why not at the same time give up smoking, drinking, and over-eating? Counselling may save you more in the long run; if it helps you to change your escapist and compensatory activities (drugs, alcohol, cigarettes, gambling, buying friends, losing jobs) it is presumably cost-effective. To pay for couple counselling to save your marriage might be worthwhile compared with the prospect of waiting months for a free service, and seeing your marriage deteriorate in the meantime. On the other hand, if you realize in advance how much a complete therapy may cost (say, £5,000) you could decide to invest in some other project, like vocational retraining or a small down payment on a flat. Only you can decide.

It is worth considering that you do not necessarily get better service by paying more: the most expensive does not necessarily equal the best. Nor do appearances: almost anyone can rent the right rooms and automatically create an impression of professional excellence; in fact, they may be no better than anyone else. You may also pay a great deal to private clinics, either on an outpatient or in-patient basis, when your counsellor is no better qualified or experienced than many others who charge quite a bit less. If you prefer to take these routes and can afford it, so be it. We are not suggesting that expensive necessarily equals 'rip-off', simply that expensive does not necessarily equal effective.

Can you take it?

Counselling can be a bumpy emotional business. It takes time and effort, in the course of which you will probably discover things about yourself you are not too keen to learn. You may be challenged to take risks, and aspects of your life may change in unpredictable ways. There are likely to be times of rewarding progress, but other times of doubt, stagnation, emptiness, or relapse. Will you remain committed in spite of such prospects?

Initially, it may be a novelty to have someone listen to you and care for you so exclusively. You may feel special, and your life may seem more manageable, or take on a different, fresh perspective. But then the novelty perhaps wears off, the fantasies you had about what you will achieve do not come true, and your therapist – who initially seemed like the embodiment of wisdom, love, and beauty – starts to look and sound ordinary, fallible, and even uncaring. You find yourself resenting the tedious sessions in which very little seems to happen. What then?

Although it is impossible to predict the course of each person's therapy, it is common for things to go up and down, for there to be highs and lows, a sense of so many steps forward and so many back. Gordon, for example, reported that in the course of four years of therapy he gained various insights and made changes in his life at certain points, but at times he seriously wondered whether he was getting anything at all from therapy. When considering therapy for yourself, you should take these troughs and peaks into account. Are you someone who will give up the moment the going gets tough? Are you looking for personal growth given to you on a plate? Will you start blaming your therapist, your wife, your boss, and everyone else when you realize that the focus is you, and any effort needed to change must also come from you?

It is common for clients to begin at some stage to resent their counsellor. Such feelings may be a replay of all the disappointments we have ever felt in relation to our parents, siblings, and other loved ones. For many people such negative emotions are an important aspect of their eventual reconciliation with the past.

Your involvement in counselling may affect your relationships generally. For many it can create friction in relationships. For example, if your partner does not support your being in counselling, this may be a difficult conflict for you. He or she may think counselling is a waste of time, or find it threatening to your relationship, or resent the amount you are spending from the family budget. The people close to you may wonder whether you are talking about them and, if so, what you are saying, and what you really think of them. These thoughts and feelings can lead to arguments or sullen silences, and may certainly make you think twice about continuing in counselling, or even about starting it.

In some cases people realize that because of what they are discovering about themselves, continuing in therapy may put them in the position of having to make unpalatable decisions, such as leaving their partners or changing careers. At such times abandoning therapy is a temptation. This is made all the harder if you realize that sometimes it *is* the therapist or the style of therapy that is wrong for you, or no longer useful. For this reason, commitment must be weighed against intelligent appraisal.

The counsellor's approach

Most counsellors and psychotherapists will have trained in one specific approach or orientation (see Chapter 6). For historical reasons there are far more psychodynamic and person-centred counsellors practising in Britain than there are representatives of other approaches.

We believe that all counsellors and psychotherapists should be willing to explain their approach to you. They should also honestly tell you if they are not likely to be able to help you, or if another therapist or counsellor would be more appropriate. This does not always happen, however.

There is now considerable evidence that certain conditions or problems are helped better by some approaches than by others. If you are experiencing panic attacks, for example, you may be helped most by a cognitive behavioural therapist; if you have longstanding relationship difficulties, you may benefit more from someone trained in the psychodynamic or person-centred tradition. A well-informed and humble practitioner should apprise you of such facts, but may not do so. Often you will have to compromise. Depending on where you live, which therapists practise there, what you can afford, and other factors you may have to see whoever you can in the hope that it will help.

Good therapists and counsellors respond with intuitive flexibility to the needs of each of their clients. You can reasonably expect to find someone to help you whether your aims are realistically broad or narrow. You cannot necessarily expect to find everything you want in one therapist at one time. If you are fortunate, you may find a good-enough therapist, someone who accompanies you a good way towards deeper meaning or higher aspirations. Again, if you are fortunate, you may find a practitioner with specific skills to help you overcome specific problems. In any case, we believe you are more likely to be lucky if you have prepared yourself with as much information as possible.

4
How Do You Find a Counsellor or Psychotherapist?

London generally has a preponderance of therapists and counsellors in private practice in comparison with the rest of the country. Large cities generally also have their fair share, and rural areas have fewest. In very remote areas you may not find one for miles around. It is also likely that certain areas are far better supplied with counsellors, psychotherapists, and psychologists in voluntary and statutory organizations than others.

Our purpose in this chapter is not primarily to discuss the geographical spread of counsellors and counselling services, but to address the questions involved in finding a practitioner for you.

Private practitioners

Directories

The British Association for Counselling Directory is probably the most comprehensive national list of practitioners, although there are other, more exclusive, lists of psychotherapists and psychologists. The United Kingdom Council for Psychotherapy (UKCP) and the British Confederation of Psychotherapy (BCP) produce annual registers of organizations and individuals meeting their criteria, for example. Counsellors generally are not included in these because many of them are not subscribers of the UKCP's or BCP's organizational members. The British Psychological Society also publishes an annual register which only includes members belonging to the Society (BPS).

The Counselling and Psychotherapy Resources Directory (CPRD), published annually by the BAC, contains the details of counsellors and therapists region by region, and has information on some voluntary and statutory agencies besides. Practitioners submit their own entries, and in many cases have to pay for entries. The fact that someone's name does not appear in the book does not mean they are not approved of by BAC; conversely, inclusion does not imply endorsement. Practitioners supply details of their contact address and/or telephone number; qualifications; professional associations; theoretical orientation; specializations; fees; and whether or not they are having supervision and therapy of their own. Anyone can use the CPRD to choose a practitioner, telephone them and begin to make arrangements. You may be able to find a copy at your local reference library, or, alternatively, contact BAC directly (see back of this book) and they will tell you or send you a list about practitioners in your area. So, is it that simple?

Like most directories, the CPRD contains the barest of information and only that supplied by practitioners themselves. It does give you some idea about who is in your locality and what the differences between them may be. But therapists go out of business, and others appear on the scene; counsellors move house or die, so this kind of information can never be entirely up to date.

The ideal directory would prove prohibitively expensive to produce, but let us fantasize for a moment about what it would contain. A photograph of the person would tell us whether it is a man or woman. This may sound obvious, but some names can be misleading, and initials are anonymous. A photograph would also indicate roughly how old someone was, whether they were black or white, and whether they looked like 'our kind of person'. Appearances can be deceptive, of course. Our ideal directory might also tell us something about the person's life, their beliefs about therapy, how long they have practised, whether they work from home or from an office, and so on.

In fact, such directories do exist in some areas where local collectives publish such details, and there are regional magazines dedicated to humanistic psychology and personal growth which carry this kind of information. Of course, such material is always self-submitted and self-promotional, so you would not expect anyone in any way to detract from an image of total profession-alism, so bear this in mind.

Readers who are completely new to the therapy business may begin to see some real difficulties emerging: you are considering parting with a lot of money and trusting a complete stranger with the most intimate details of your life; don't you need to know what you're getting into? The CPRD is an excellent resource, and we have known many people to use it with satisfactory results, but all such routes have an element of searching in the dark about them.

Advertising

You can, of course, consider the Yellow Pages. Advertisements for counsellors and psychotherapists carry the barest of information, sometimes only a name and telephone number. Some are more commercially oriented and carry slogans and testimonies. There is simply no way of knowing what sort of person or practitioner is behind the advertisement. In certain magazines advertisers have to clear the hurdle of submitting photocopied certificates and diplomas before their ad is printed.

You will also see advertisements in shop windows, on business cards, leaflets, and posters. Since in recent years a large number of people have been training as counsellors and psychotherapists, competition has begun to increase, and there has been a commensurate increase in advertising. Some training institutes either prohibit or discourage such advertising, relying instead on referrals from the parent institute to graduate and affiliated practitioners. This might lead you to think that only those practitioners who do *not* advertise are to be respected and trusted; unfortunately, this is not a reliable guide.

Organizations

If you have decided, however, that you definitely want a well-defined practitioner, say, a psychoanalyst, psychoanalytical psychotherapist, transactional analyst, Gestalt therapist, or similar, it does make sense to contact the training institutes. You can ask for an assessment interview, or, if you live a long way from them, a direct referral to a local practitioner. By going to an organization, you have some assurance that if you are unhappy with the treatment you received, you have some means of complaining. You might also feel reassured by knowing that a professional body is involved, rather than only an individual. You can ask the training organizations if they have trainees willing to see you at low cost. Consider writing to several organizations and asking for their brochures; in this way, you can decide in a leisurely way which ones appeal to you. The addresses of some of these can be found at the back of this book (note that inclusion does not imply endorsement).

Word of mouth

You would probably not have to ask around very widely to learn the names of some of your local therapists. By asking friends, colleagues, GPs, social workers, youth and community workers, nurses, community psychiatric nurses (CPNs), ministers of religion, health visitors and community centres you will soon begin to find out who is known in your area.

Make a list of the names you are given, and, if you can, find out something about them. Ask how long they have practised in the area, whether they specialize, where they work from, and anything else that will help build a profile. Decide what you would really like to know – Do they have feminist sympathies? Do they have experience of eating disorders? Do they come from your part of the world? – and then ask your questions. The more you ask around, the more likely you are to hear the same name several times, a positive recommendation. If you live in a large city it is more difficult to get local recommendations, but you can still try to identify practitioners about whom your friends and others know something.

You may know a counsellor or therapist personally whom you can ask about suitable colleagues. The problem here, however, is that practitioners tend naturally enough to recommend their friends and close colleagues, and are not necessarily familiar with their work and how good they are, or to be aware of other options.

If you have friends who have been or are still in therapy, they might be willing to tell you something about the therapist. Some people, however, consider their therapy and their therapist a private area of their life, so tread with care. Quite often people decide to visit the same counsellor as a friend. This has its problems, however, as some practitioners are not willing to see people who know each other – and your friend may not want to share his or her counsellor with you! Furthermore, although your friend may think her counsellor is the best thing since sliced bread, this is no guarantee that they are the best person for you. How attractive and easy to relate to we find other people is quite an idiosyncratic business; probably, as often as not, we cannot understand what our friend sees in so-and-so. One of the people we interviewed went to see a new therapist after being recommended by a friend. He quickly realized he was not at all comfortable with this therapist, and, as well as having to endure several weeks of uncertainty and discomfort, he started to feel uncomfortable about his friend and to question her judgement.

As with anything, relying on the recommendations of friends can backfire.

One person we know, on seeing a therapist in action as a workshop leader, decided subsequently to seek therapy from him. She was sorely disappointed when she discovered that the therapist, who had seemed so able and charismatic as a teacher, in a one-to-one situation behaved coolly and was quite off-putting. You may think you need certain qualities in a therapist, yet when you get them you may realize that your choice was based on an old fantasy or a misplaced idea. Sometimes what we are searching for is an ideal person who does not exist. Perhaps we would be better off with someone completely unknown.

Clearly the subject of how to identify a counsellor with whom you can work productively is problematic. Surprisingly little has been researched or written in this area; this is all the more surprising when you consider that the therapeutic relationship is widely believed to be a crucial – if not *the* most crucial – factor in the success of any form of psychotherapy.

Getting started

Suppose that by one means or another you come up with the names of half-a-dozen contenders. We suggest you then make a short-list. From the information available, which are the likeliest three therapists? Who do you like the sound of? Who appears to be well qualified? Whose address is most convenient for you? Who seems best equipped to help you with your particular problem? Who is within your price range? Would you prefer to see a man or a woman? See if you can then rank these in order of preference. Include in your thinking some questions about who may be best for you objectively. You may like the sound of one because she seems nice, and steer clear of another because you sense she is a no-nonsense type. Try to make a balanced choice.

It is recommended that you arrange to speak to on the telephone or meet two or three counsellors before committing yourself to one (the next chapter deals with what exactly you should ask the counsellor). Many counsellors would expect you to do this, and would certainly not feel offended by the idea: you are simply trying to get an idea of who may be most helpful to you, depending on their expertise, approach, availability, fees, and suitability. Some counsellors will gladly see you for a first meeting with no commitment, and sometimes with no payment.

At this stage you may be tempted to back out of the whole thing, but try to push yourself a little. For many people this shopping-around process is far from easy. Particularly if your problems include unassertiveness, shyness, and a desire to please – common enough difficulties – you may not feel able to bring yourself to 'interview' several people and reject most of them! It is best to be as brave as possible – but if you simply cannot bring yourself to make the phone calls, it is preferable to get a friend to help you than to put up with continuing distress, although the counsellor will take note of your difficulty in asking for help.

Free and low-cost counselling

Free or low-fee counselling and psychotherapy delivered within the voluntary and statutory sectors is not inferior to that provided by private practitioners, for which you pay more. Those who work privately choose to do so for their own reasons, and many of them also work part-time in organizations. Some choose to offer their services in both the private and voluntary sectors, because they enjoy and believe in working with people from all sections of society. Some for political reasons refuse to work privately and regard themselves as committed to free public health care.

Margaret lost both her parents some years ago, lives alone and sometimes feels quite depressed. She has little money to spare, but decides she would like to try counselling or therapy. She talks to her GP about this, and he says that unfortunately his practice does not have a counsellor attached to it. He can refer her for an assessment appointment at the out-patient psycho-therapy clinic locally, but the waiting-list is known to be at least a year. He could get a community psychiatric nurse to see her, who could possibly arrange counselling. Alternatively, there are one or two mental health agencies locally which have counselling services, but he is unsure about their quality. There are also, he says, some self-help groups. What will Margaret do?

We use this example because it illustrates the common dilemma faced by someone who seeks counselling but cannot pay for it. It also raises the point that such services may vary enormously in quality and availability from area to area. We now go on to look at some of the variety of free and low-cost services available.

GPs and the NHS

You should consult your GP first about any distress or emotional disturbance you are experiencing because such problems may have organic causes. Many GPs now have counsellors, and sometimes psychotherapists, attached to their practices. This is a growing trend, but it depends very much on your doctor's attitude towards counselling. Ask your GP if there is any such service and if not, if it is possible to be referred to a similar service elsewhere. Idiosyncratic arrangements from one area or one GP to another mean that you could be lucky enough to be put in touch quickly with a counsellor, psychotherapist, clinical psychologist, or community psychiatric nurse who can offer you counselling.

Due to scarcity of resources, you may find that such services have a long waiting-list, or that you can only have a limited number of sessions. If you are offered brief or time-limited counselling, however, do not assume that it cannot help you; it may be all you need, or it may prove an excellent starting point, as we discuss below.

Bear in mind that some GPs will reach for the prescription pad when you mention depression or anxiety, so you need to be able to say you would prefer to try counselling instead of medication. You also have certain rights as an NHS-user; do not be afraid to ask assertively about services which you know to be available.

Besides asking your GP directly, you can find out if psychotherapy and clinical psychology services are available in your area by investigating at your local reference library, or asking at a local community mental health centre. Sometimes there are specific services for specific problems, such as eating disorders, phobias, obsessions, sexual or relationship problems, and so on. Some hospital-based clinical psychology services accept self-referrals in such cases. We know of at least one NHS facility which offers an excellent clinical psychology service which is also linked with a counselling course. This service refers people with less serious concerns to trainee counsellors with minimal waiting time. People with more serious or complicated problems in this service are seen by psychologists, who may also assess others less seriously troubled as being likely to benefit from a less specific counselling facility. However, there are often long waiting-lists for such help.

Brief therapies

It is partly because of such problems with waiting-lists that a purpose-designed, time-limited (16 sessions) therapy was developed at Guy's and St Thomas' Hospitals in London. Known as cognitive-analytic therapy (CAT), this has the merit of reducing waiting-lists somewhat, and attempting to offer a disciplined form of help which looks both at underlying factors and at present crises. This and similar models are being utilized and researched, and gradually are being offered more widely. Another project, aimed at reducing waiting-lists has been developed at the University of Sheffield. Known as the two-plus-one model, it is based on research which suggests that people are often most helped by the first one or two sessions, followed by time, reflection, and action. It has been found that certain people prefer and benefit from such short-term help rather than ongoing therapy. Brief therapy is particularly suited for people with clear-cut problems for which there are specific goals, and who have the personal resources to take an active role in the brief time that therapy lasts. We mention these two examples because the general public is probably unaware that such efforts are being made, and that in certain areas these models are available as free services.

Student counselling

Counselling in the educational sector is one of the best established parts of counselling activity in this country. Standards are very high, and services are not usually time-limited.

It is recognized that young people making the transition from home to a completely new environment, experiencing academic pressures and often identity crises, are a vulnerable group. In many areas of the country there are statutory youth counselling projects addressing problems in this age group such as parental conflict, drugs, unexpected pregnancies, and so on.

If you are a student in higher education, your college or university almost certainly has a free counselling service. Some university counselling services are available to staff as well as students, and therefore cover thousands of potential clients. Even if you are not a student, it can be worth contacting such services to ask for recommendations for similar services.

Employee counselling

In the commercial sector too there is a growing trend for organizations to provide staff counselling and welfare services, free of charge, to employees. Sometimes known as employee assistance programmes, these services usually offer prompt, time-limited, face-to-face or telephone counselling to staff of all grades, as well as their immediate families. Often, they also provide legal and financial advice and information, and may also help you to investigate alternative sources of assistance.

Such services are confidential, and clients do not have to bring only work-related problems. Some of the banks, building societies, public transport services, and retail chains have special counselling available to staff who are exposed to violent assaults and armed raids. Many clients use these services for exactly the kinds of personal issues – depression, anxiety, relationship difficulties – which are also addressed by counsellors in GPs' surgeries and in student health services.

It is worth checking whether your employer is involved in any such schemes, or would consider becoming involved. Employers sometimes are willing to sponsor an employee for personal counselling, allowing them time off work, or even paying their fees.

The voluntary sector

This includes many small-scale, grass roots, self-help groups; larger, well-established, mutual-aid organizations; and well-known, often partially state-funded agencies. It is always worth considering whether these are an option for you, especially if your problem is primarily drug- or drink-related. Narcotics Anonymous and Alcoholics Anonymous help a great many people free of charge, and there is little if any evidence that they are less effective than professional services. There are no waiting-lists and no charges, and there is a great deal of support offered. You will have to decide whether you are prepared to enter the kinds of group situation, which may have a religious dimension, that such organizations provide. Many satisfied members testify that they were not helped in one-to-one counselling because they needed the support and pressure of fellow sufferers.

The best-known specialist voluntary organizations are probably Relate, Samaritans, Cruse, Victim Support, and MIND. These deal, respectively, with relationships; depression and suicidal feelings; bereavement; the psychological, physical, and legal consequences of suffering criminal assaults and injuries; and mental illness.

Relate offers counselling to heterosexual and homosexual couples, and to single people with relationship problems. The focus of counselling is always the relationship, but may include discussion of individual, deep-seated problems. Donations are welcomed, and guidelines sometimes suggest a fair level for these. Relate counsellors include volunteers with basic training, and highly trained and experienced counsellors.

Samaritans refer to their service as listening therapy and telephone befriending. They conduct their service mainly by telephone, although some branches have face-to-face counselling facilities. Samaritans is not simply an end-of-the-road facility for people about to kill themselves. Calls are also received and welcomed from people who are lonely, isolated, depressed, or generally distressed with no one else to turn to. Sometimes people in psychotherapy or counselling will be told about their local Samaritans in case of emergency distress between sessions, or when their therapist may be unavailable. Samaritans are carefully selected and trained for their telephone work.

Cruse Bereavement Care is for people who have suffered a bereavement and need help coming to terms with it. Their volunteer staff arrange to visit the person in their own home, and to continue to visit by appointment until they feel able to cope alone, or with the help of friends and family.

Like the counsellors working with Cruse, those trained within Victim Support visit people at home. If the person has suffered a recent crime, they are usually prepared to give them information about their rights, to accompany them to court, and to provide basic counselling.

Many such organizations vary in what they offer from local branch to branch. This is also true of MIND, which may offer support and advocacy services for people with serious mental health problems, lunch clubs, and even housing. Many local MIND branches have free or low-cost counselling services for members of the local community, and sometimes specific services for people from ethnic minority groups.

Many religious organizations provide counselling and psychotherapy services. Religious commitment is not necessarily required. The Westminster Pastoral Foundation (WPF), in existence for over 25 years, provides counselling and therapy, usually at low cost, and also runs high-quality counselling training courses. The Salvation Army, Catholic, Methodist, Jewish, and other groups offer a number of general and specialist counselling facilities, either at no cost or by requesting donations. Counsellors in these organizations range from those with many years' experience, to counsellors in training who offer their work free to the organization in return for experience and, sometimes, supervision.

Some of the smaller organizations of this kind do not publicize themselves but rely on word of mouth to become known. You may therefore find there are such services near to where you live if you begin to investigate. In some cases, even if you do not live nearby, you may still be seen.

Counselling for ethnic minority and religious groups

If you belong to an ethnic minority or a specific religious group, you may want or need counselling from someone who shares your beliefs and traditions. You may need to find a counsellor or therapist who literally speaks the same language as you. You have the right to express your preference for a counsellor who is black, who speaks your language, or understands your religion and culture. Even if no one is available who matches these needs, you will be helping the organization to identify your needs and to attempt to provide the best help possible.

Unfortunately, therapy centres like Nafsiyat in London and the Asian Family Counselling Service in Bradford are rare. There are signs, however, that awareness is growing into the specific needs of minority communities. Counsellors generally are becoming aware that they need to sensitize themselves to cultural issues.

The Commission for Racial Equality published a booklet about the experiences of depression of Asian women (*The Sorrow in my Heart*) which describes the problems for and special needs of Asian clients. We know of people of Asian origin who have established services of their own and organized translation services to help non-English-speaking people benefit from urgent counselling.

If you fall into one of these groups, you might consider contacting any groups that have established themselves, wherever they are, and ask for contacts in your area, or, alternatively for advice about how to begin your own service.

Specialist counselling and therapy

Part of your search for what is best for and available to you will involve identifying whether your concerns are specialist in any way. There are many counselling agencies which provide specialist help associated with HIV and AIDS, abortion, medication, sexual abuse, lesbian and gay problems, rare diseases, debt, redundancy, post-traumatic stress, and so on. Some have a branch in every major city and town, others are based only in London. You may need a free service, or particular expertise and protection. There are centres, for example, that provide residential help. Most public reference libraries have directories which can help you to find organizations like these. Remember, you can always try something out, and if it does not work, you can have another try. But if you are experiencing acute distress, pain, or confusion, get help and advice immediately from your doctor.

5
What Should You Ask?

If you are contacting a private therapist, it will almost certainly begin with an exploratory phone call. Often you will encounter an answering machine because the therapist may be busy seeing someone else. Do leave a message or be persistent in calling back.

Before you speak, you should have your questions prepared, in writing if need be. What is your opening line? How will the conversation proceed?

Client: Hello, is that Susan Jones? My name's Harry Harkness and I'm interested in seeing a counsellor. Do you have any vacancies at the moment?

Counsellor: I do, yes.

Client: Well, can I just ask you a few things first?

Counsellor: Of course.

Client: I get quite depressed and I think I need to talk about things. I've been through quite a lot in the last few years. Do you help people who are depressed?

Counsellor: I've worked with depressed people, yes.

Client: Can you tell me how much your fees are?

Counsellor: They're £28 an hour.

Client: Oh, I see. And, er, do you live anywhere near a bus route?

This brief conversation – which is not necessarily typical – begins to illustrate the kinds of difficulties that can arise even at this early stage. It is sensible to ask straight away if the counsellor has any vacancies, or is still practising, otherwise you may be wasting your time. You are not obliged to start talking about the nature of your problems, although you may wish to start talking straight away. Sometimes you will be discouraged from saying too much, and will instead be invited to arrange an exploratory face-to-face meeting.

It is sensible to ask the counsellor if they can help with specific problems, although some are not interested in, or do not believe in the usefulness of, diagnostic categories. If you say that your problem is depression and the counsellor replies that her expertise lies in helping victims of sexual abuse, you may wonder, as she may, whether there will be a good fit. It also makes sense to ask about fees because you could be wasting your time if they are completely beyond your means. You will need to have in mind just how much you can afford or are prepared to pay; if the counsellor states a figure that is completely beyond you, you can politely terminate the conversation, or ask whether the fees are negotiable. Depending on where you live and your mobility, it may be important to find out how accessible the counsellor is for you in terms of distance and transport. If you have mobility problems relating to a disability you will also need to ask about disabled access.

As well as exchanging information with each other, you will get an impression from the counsellor's tone of voice, its warmth or otherwise, degree of friendliness or formality, articulateness, humour, and so on. While he or she may answer your questions satisfactorily, they may convey non-verbally something that you do not warm to; conversely, they may say nothing very remarkable, yet sound very caring and likeable. Since these kinds of qualities tend to be important in forming a good working alliance with your potential counsellor, you would do well to note them.

Some counsellors have typewritten information sheets about themselves and their services which they can send to you in advance. If this is not offered, ask whether anything like it is available, and if there is time to receive it before a first appointment.

Your first appointment

Suppose you have made your first appointment. You arrive at the counsellor's consulting room. The counsellor may well know what he or she wants to ask you – but what are you going to ask them? Do you know if this first session is to be charged at full cost, or at all? Do you know how long it is to be – 50 minutes, 60 minutes, or longer? Would you prefer to spend it gaining information from the counsellor or launching straight into your pressing concerns? We will imagine for the sake of illustration that you are perfectly in command of yourself and ready to interview the counsellor exhaustively. You might want to ask some of the questions below.

Bear in mind that if you were actually to read through such a list, or to recite it from memory, most counsellors would be either astonished or highly suspicious. It would certainly not sound very trusting of you if you were literally to go through the entire inventory, and we are not suggesting that you do this. Some of these questions may be crucial for you, while others may not be of interest. Also, you may ask what is most important now, and find out the rest later. In some cases, the counsellor will not have thought about some of these issues before – or will not have been confronted by such an informed consumer.

Some first-meeting questions

- Are you fully qualified?
- What are your qualifications?
- To which code of ethics do you subscribe?
- Is everything I say completely confidential?
- How long have you been practising?
- Do you specialize in any particular area?
- Do you have experience with my specific problems?
- What is your theoretical orientation?
- How firmly do you adhere to this approach?
- To what extent are you flexible and eclectic in your approach?
- What does the research say about the effectiveness of your approach with my particular problem?
- Are you willing to explain what you are doing and thinking as we go along?
- How long do you think I will be seeing you?
- Will I see you on a regular, weekly basis? Can I have shorter, longer or more or less frequent sessions if I find that helpful?
- What is your cancellation policy?
- Do you charge clients if their holidays don't coincide with yours? How much notice would you like?
- Can I call you between sessions if I need to? Is there any charge for this?
- Can my partner come along at some stage?

- How much do you charge? Is that fixed or negotiable?
- What happens if I am made redundant?
- How do you prefer to be paid? (Cheque or cash; weekly or monthly; at the beginning or end of sessions)
- Can I smoke?
- Can I tape record our sessions?
- How should I address you?
- May I say if I don't think things are going well?
- Will I be asked to record dreams, keep a diary, or do homework?
- Will you tell me if at any point you think you can't help me?

What you ask and how you ask it will be partly determined by your personality, level of assertiveness, state of mind, feelings about authority and knowledge of your rights. While you are hoping that the therapist is going to be able to help you, you are also about to help them pay part of their mortgage! Although we make this point humorously, remember that counsellors are in business – it is how they earn their living – and need to protect their reputation.

They know also they must observe their codes of practice. If you are unsure about your rights, do ask the counsellor for a copy of their code of ethics, or ask where you can get one. Ideally, the counsellor will spend time with you going through a code of ethics. The *BAC Code of Ethics and Practice for Counsellors*, for example, is a very comprehensive document which deals with issues of competency and accountability.

Counsellors should provide clear contracting and should make it clear what their qualifications are. We know of one or two cases where barely trained practitioners have set up in private practice and have not necessarily announced their, shall we say, lack of experience. If you do not ask questions about qualifications and experience, you may have no idea whose hands you are in. (This is not an indictment of newly trained counsellors, most of whom are very competent.)

As well as asking 'personal' questions about qualifications and so on, you need to have simple, practical information. If you work irregular hours as a shiftworker, for example, you need to establish whether your therapist can make flexible appointments. Some therapists believe that it is important to adhere to the same appointment time every week. If this is the case, will you try to negotiate, or will you try to change your shifts?

Asking questions for different reasons

Many potential clients are afraid of what could be in store for them in their counselling, and many, quite naturally, are somewhat shy and anxious when entering a strange situation for the first time. You might try to hide your shyness or anxiety behind a barrage of questions. Since much of the process of counselling depends on trust, sooner or later you will have to trust your counsellor. Asking someone what their qualifications are may be a perfectly straightforward request because you want to establish whether this is the right counsellor for you. However, such a question may be asked by someone who mistrusts everyone around them; the counsellor or therapist will not know you well enough to determine what has motivated you. They will, however, be considering both possibilities.

The best use of questions is to clarify practical and contractual matters. Certain matters are more complex. For example, confidentiality may not be guaranteed to be complete, if the counsellor must discuss their work with their supervisors. Other people, such as your GP, may need to be notified, because the counsellor does not have medical training, in order to safeguard you and others should your behaviour ever become dangerous to yourself or others. Most counsellors keep notes and records of their work, and you may wish to clarify what right of access you have. You may also like to know how these records are secured.

Questions like 'Am I mad?' or 'Am I beyond hope?' are far from unusual. People often wonder if they are crazy, or so troubled that they may not be capable of benefiting from counselling or psychotherapy. If you are in real distress, a direct answer may be the most helpful. Do not be surprised, however, if your therapist simply says, 'Do *you* think you're mad?' or, 'You'd like me to tell you if you're mad or not.'

Most counsellors and psychotherapists are not medically or psychiatrically trained, and they would not therefore be in a position to give a categorical answer to such a question. Anyone who is seriously, clinically disturbed is unlikely to have the presence of mind to put the question so clearly and openly. We believe, however, you deserve some indication from your therapist or counsellor of their view on this. When your question is reflected back at you, the intention is not to be baffling or evasive, but to encourage you to evaluate your own mental state and your own ability to recover, or perhaps to find out what 'madness' means for you.

Questions which you put directly to your counsellor that involve decisions you face (Should I do this or that?) may well be genuine but will usually not be answered directly. The ethos of counselling and psychotherapy rests on a fundamental respect for each person's ability to do their own thinking and come to their own conclusions. Counsellors do not think of themselves as advisers, although some are concerned to help you solve your immediate moral and practical dilemmas.

If you are gay, you might feel it is crucial to be counselled by someone who is also gay. If you ask the counsellor if they are gay, and he or she does not answer directly it is because it is usually the intention of the counsellor to get you to trust your *own* thinking about these matters, rather than to rely on another's views or status. Sometimes therapists and counsellors may decide they can be more helpful to you if certain matters are not discussed. If you become highly entangled in intellectual exchanges with your therapist, your original concerns may get overshadowed. However, only you can decide which of your concerns are peripheral to you, and which are central.

In some of the more behavioural, task-centred forms of counselling and therapy, where there is less emphasis on the relationship with the therapist as the prime therapeutic factor, you may be less inclined to ask personal questions of the therapist. If you are seeing a clinical psychologist or psychotherapist it is probable that you can take for granted the qualifications of a practitioner in such settings, although some out-patient NHS psychotherapy services use therapists who are still in training. It may be pointless asking for flexible appointment times if you have to take what you are offered. You are entitled, however, to be asked to give your informed consent about proposed treatment plans, so do not refrain from asking for an explanation for your therapist's procedures.

The advent of patients' charters and official complaints

procedures means that you have recourse to being heard by employing authorities if you are unhappy with the treatment you receive.

In conclusion, let us remind you that it helps to be prepared. What do you absolutely *need* to know about your counsellor? If you feel at all shy or intimidated about asking certain questions, you might preface them with, 'Do you mind if I ask you something?' Finally, no matter what your problem is, or what state of mind you may be in, value yourself enough to find out what you are getting into, whether it is right for you, and whether your counsellor or therapist is treating you humanely, openly, and effectively.

6
What Are the Different Approaches to Counselling and Therapy?

Psychoanalysis, psychotherapy, hypnotherapy, Gestalt therapy, transactional analysis, cognitive therapy, neuro-linguistic programming, primal therapy, person-centred therapy – most people will have heard enough different names in the field of therapy to be aware that it can be a confusing subject area. It has been calculated that there are more than 300 different approaches to therapy and counselling. Even an attempt to identify the mainstream therapeutic approaches in Britain alone cannot reduce the field to less than about ten approaches. One can respond to this multiplicity of types of counselling and therapy either with fascination or scepticism – or both. To make sense of so many specialist approaches would involve an apparently formidable amount of reading and study! We hope in this chapter to be able to guide you through this maze.

There are many theoretical approaches to therapy. These are often referred to as 'theoretical orientations'. There are also a number of contexts in which therapy is conducted: individual, couple, family, and group therapy or counselling. Although individual counselling is the most common, the others are practised fairly extensively. There are also specialisms, such as child psychotherapy and sex therapy; brief and long-term therapies; complementary therapies; and a number of attempts to join approaches together, known as eclectic or integrative approaches.

Critics of therapy often dismiss all these different approaches and their languages as 'psycho-babble', and as nothing more than confusing brand names for the same product. This is not accurate. Therapy cannot be compared with petrol, for example, one brand of which seems pretty much identical to another, with only the packaging and names being different. Each of the major therapeutic approaches represents a fundamentally different philosophy of life; each may be suited to certain individuals but not to others; many are in open conflict with each other.

Although there is research that suggests that little distinguishes one approach from another in terms of how successful it is, this does not mean that what is practised is not distinctive. Certain methods, for example, are characterized by conversation, while others are inclined towards activity, emotional expression, or physical contact. What some practitioners consider essential for effective therapy, others find anathema. If you are venturing into the territory of psychotherapy and counselling for the first time, be prepared to read and hear about many conflicting claims and explanations, many of which, unfortunately, are unhelpful to those who are distressed, perplexed, and in need of help. You need to identify precisely which orientation may best help you.

The different therapeutic approaches

This is not the place to go into the history of psychotherapy and counselling, but it is useful to remember that psychoanalysis began about 100 years ago with Sigmund Freud. Classical Freudian psychoanalysis gradually evolved and split into a number of variants, beginning with psychoanalytical psychotherapy. A number of psychoanalytically trained practitioners over the years broke away from their Freudian origins and founded their own schools: Jung (analytical psychology); Adler (individual psychology); Perls (Gestalt therapy); Assagioli (psychosynthesis); Berne (transactional analysis or TA); Ellis (rational emotive behaviour therapy); Beck (cognitive therapy); Janov (primal therapy); and many others. Although many of the founders of these groups had similar theoretical roots, their approaches to therapy are far from being similar to each other. Many fall broadly within what is known as 'humanistic psychology'. The following are very brief sketches of some of the important therapies. The way we have chosen to describe these will probably not meet with the approval of all practitioners. Hopefully, we are presenting a fair description in a very confined space of what are often complex processes.

In our research interviews we heard both satisfied and dissatisfied accounts of experiences. Practitioners sometimes defend their own schools by arguing that dissatisfied clients may have been unfortunate enough to have worked with poorly trained or maverick therapists. Our own view is that in all schools you may meet practitioners whose personalities do not mesh well with your own; equally, in all schools there are probably practitioners who are not able to adapt sufficiently to different clients' needs and personalities.

Psychoanalytic Approaches

These include classical Freudian psychoanalysis (or simply 'analysis'); psychoanalytic psychotherapy; communicative analysis; Lacanian analysis; micro-analysis; psychodynamic counselling, as well as attempts to blend elements from two or more of these together. It is debatable whether or not Jung, the Jungians, and post-Jungians belong here. Although they are generally regarded as belonging in the same 'depth psychology' camp as other analysts, their focus is often quite different.

Most psychoanalytic approaches share the view that there is a powerful part of our psyche called the unconscious, which reveals itself in dreams, slips of the tongue, forgetfulness, jokes, psychosomatic symptoms, and in other ways. The psyche also contains the id, (the uncontrolled, primitive mind); the ego (the realistic, balancing mind); and the super-ego (the repressive, parental mind). According to this approach we are in conflict all our lives. Not only are we born with insatiable, demanding instincts, but also we suffer from maternal absences and shortcomings, and from competition with our parents and siblings.

A typical psychoanalytically trained practitioner encourages the client during a session to sink into his or her own inner thoughts and feelings and to say whatever comes to mind. The therapist may be somewhat withdrawn, allowing the client to express anything he or she wishes, and to arrive at most of their own conclusions. Other analysts prefer a more naturalistic interaction. There is a rationale for both positions, but it is not easy to separate therapists' personalities – and their shortcomings – from their theoretical rationales; an excellent and effective therapist may be purposefully detached from you, but, equally, a therapist may be detached because that is his or her habitual behaviour.

In the course of therapy, you may come to feel your therapist is wonderful and you cannot live without them; or you may resent them and think they are inadequate, spiteful, cold, and so on. The therapist will allow, and even encourage, you to experience and express such feelings, and in time will help you to see that they are really about your parents and significant others. The general aim of such approaches is that by freely expressing all feelings and thoughts you will uncover more and more of your unconscious. Gradually, as you become aware of these, you will become less fixed in rigid patterns of thought, feeling, and behaviour derived from the past, and thus more available for full experience of the present.

> Susan had tried one or two therapists and counsellors but had been unhappy with the pressure to change that she felt with them. She chose to see a psychoanalytical psychotherapist. Her thrice-weekly therapy lasted for several years. Gradually and painstakingly she was able to look at the many strands of good and bad influences in her past and present. With time, Susan came to trust her own thoughts and feelings, to understand her mood changes, and to let go of many regrets and distorted expectations. While little appeared to change in Susan's outer life, she felt generally much more content and in possession of herself.

How can you decide whether this kind of approach might be best for you? It is usually a long-term method (years rather than weeks or months), and often requires attendance several times a week. The therapist will be consistent: you can be sure that the same person will always be there, reliably, ready to hear you and to understand what you say in relation to all your stories and statements over the course of months and years. Except in its intensive, brief-psychotherapy formats, it is an unhurried approach and allows plenty of space for reflection, thinking aloud, wandering into and recalling memories, exploring dreams, and expressing highly idiosyncratic yet liberating thoughts. If you know or suspect that there are things in your past – remembered or not – that are affecting your life, you may opt for this kind of approach. Particularly if you have suffered emotional traumas, like childhood sexual abuse or early loss, you may prefer its gradualness.

Critics of the psychoanalytic method claim it is often far too long, too expensive, and that there is little evidence for its effectiveness. Analysts, they say, encourage dependency, and pay too much attention to the past and too little to current-life difficulties. Analysis and its variants are sometimes seen as élitist because, being generally very expensive, especially over a long period of time, it is an option only for those who can afford it. It is seldom available within free services, except on training pro-grammes, where the supervised trainee students will see clients for reduced fees. It is also sometimes said that analysts falsely convince themselves and their clients that only highly trained analysts are really qualified to understand and interpret the nuances of clients' material. In spite of all such criticisms, psychodynamic therapy and counselling is widely practised in Britain; you may take comfort from the belief that thousands of therapists and their clients cannot be totally wrong.

Behavioural, rational emotive, and cognitive-behavioural approaches

From the discipline of psychology, with its distinctively scientific orientation, has come behaviourism and the various forms of behaviour therapy. These approaches stem from a desire to measure human behaviour in some way that allows for accurate measurement of changes in behaviour. Behaviour therapy for some time was not concerned with the workings of the human psyche, but confined itself to studying only what was observable (some of what has been learned in behaviour therapy comes from experiments with animals; this is probably one of the reasons why some people dislike it).

This has changed in recent years with the advent of various kinds of cognitive-behaviour therapy, which, as the name implies, is concerned with the thinking part of human behaviour. Cognitive-behaviour therapies focus on difficulties in thinking, mood, and behaviour. Their aim is to identify each client's typical and situational styles of irrational or distorted thinking, and to help them to change this to more realistic styles, with better adaptation to everyday life.

Behaviour therapy is often associated with the study and treatment of particular, well-defined psychological disturbances, such as panic attacks, phobias, and obsessional behaviour. Although behaviour therapy has had its fair share of dissidents and break-away groups, it is probably less disparate than some other broad approaches. Within the behavioural tradition, atten-tion has been paid to social-learning theory, which includes observations and theories about the origins of some psychological disturbances.

The overriding thesis in behaviour therapy is that we learn certain unhelpful behaviour patterns in childhood and adulthood, and we need to unlearn them or replace them with others in order to improve our functioning. We may pick up certain behaviour patterns simply by watching our parents and others, and later fail to note that some of these patterns are no longer helpful. We may create for ourselves unhelpful responses to stressful situations, for example biting our nails, which we later find almost impossible to change. Sometimes our behaviour changes dramatically following a single traumatic experience. Sometimes we deal poorly with social situations because nobody has ever taught us how to deal with them effectively.

Most behaviour therapists have a minimal interest in exploring the details of clients' biographies. They want to know what the precise problematic behaviour is; how long it has been going on; in what situations it occurs; how intense it is; and whether other family members have similar problems (it is known, for example, that many varieties of anxiety are family traits). Because of its precise focus, behaviour therapy lends itself to the treatment of well-defined disturbances or problems such as phobias, aversions, anxiety states, obsessive-compulsive disorders (hand-washing, shoplifting, and so on), and certain sexual problems (premature ejaculation).

Behaviour therapy is characterized by a clear treatment plan in which the client plays an active part. You will be required to do certain things; you may be taught certain procedures; your therapist may accompany you to places associated with your problems. You may be offered an intensive, confrontational form of treatment. For example, if you are afraid of travelling in lifts, forcing yourself to use one 20 times a day for three weeks may be the solution. Alternatively, with the method known as 'systematic desensitization' you are gradually exposed to the feared object or situation. Often this will be accompanied by relaxation training, or how to calm yourself by using certain breathing techniques.

The cognitive-behavioural approaches include cognitive therapy, rational emotive behaviour therapy, problem-solving therapy, and stress inoculation training. To an extent, multi-modal therapy, reality therapy, and brief solution-focused therapy might be included under this category. You may have heard little about cognitive-behavioural approaches because they are newer than the psychoanalytic tradition, and also because they are less easily found among private practitioners; you are more likely to be offered them within the NHS, or you may have to ask about their availability.

What all these approaches have in common are the central concepts that thinking, feeling and behaviour affect one another, but that we are not bound to feel miserable when certain events occur; rather, we tend to have our own beliefs and interpretations about events which distort things. For example, someone speaks sharply to me, and I then convince myself that everyone hates me. The cognitive behaviourist believes that we typically have certain longstanding views about life and the way it should be – when it is not that way – and that we constantly, actively upset ourselves by believing that people must like us, life must be fair, we absolutely should not have to work hard, and so on. Rigid and unrealistic thinking leads to unhappiness and passivity.

In rational emotive behaviour therapy (REBT) you are taught to recognize how your own thinking upsets you emotionally; gradually you learn to become adept at identifying your self-defeating thoughts, and to replace them with realistic ones. Combined with challenging tasks to help you overcome your irrational beliefs, REBT is a method which you can use in all areas of your life as a way of re-educating and challenging yourself.

In cognitive-behavioural approaches there is often a combination of educational elements; challenging existing thought patterns; understanding more helpful kinds of thinking; assignments done between sessions; and discouragement of dependency on the therapist or counsellor. The emphasis is on getting better rather than on talking about it or getting temporary relief; on practising new behaviour in the here and now rather than hoping it will just happen.

Like behaviour therapy, cognitive-behaviour therapy tends to focus on specific problems, but unlike behaviour therapy there is a great deal of potential for putting what is learned to extensive use in many areas of life; social inhibitions can be challenged and changed; general themes can be identified and worked on, both in and out of counselling, for example, guilt, shame, shyness, and depression. Some research indicates that cognitive-behaviour therapy may have the edge over other therapies in the treatment of depression and anxiety. This may be because in its focus on current psychological problems it provides some degree of rapid progress, and therefore, real hope.

Bernard, a man of 28, began experiencing panic attacks after his partner left him. He believed he could not cope without him, and began to anticipate inordinate difficulties in everyday situations. A cognitive-behavioural therapist suggested Bernard keep a diary of his negative thoughts. By exploring these often irrational thoughts, considering more rational ones, and deliberately exposing himself to stressful situations, Bernard overcame his panic, and learned to live without the distressing belief that he could not live alone.

While the psychodynamic or analytic method is about the unconscious, interpersonal dynamics and imagery, memory and reflection – finding out and understanding *why* you feel as you do – behavioural theory and methods are about observable problematic behaviour and task-setting: direct attempts at changing behaviour patterns in specific, current areas of the client's life. Behaviour therapists do not look for answers in the client's psyche; instead, they work directly with symptoms. It is this which earns them criticism from those who believe that our psychological problems stem from underlying conflicts: by simply removing the symptoms of the conflict, all you achieve is temporary relief, which will probably be followed by the outbreak of yet more symptoms.

Critics also say that behaviour therapists belong to a medically oriented tradition in which 'doctor knows best'; hence, the negative epithet 'directive' will often be heard in connection with these approaches. It is said that behaviour therapists are cold, scientific, and uninterested in relating to their clients. Practitioners are also said to be impoverished because they emphasize only action and thinking and leave feelings, imagination, and spirituality out of the picture. Critics have also said that any success is owed to common sense; some behaviourists are quite happy to accept this, stating that they are pleased to be able to use applied common sense to human suffering – others insist that cognitive-behavioural therapists are strictly scientific.

But what does this debate mean to you, if you are acutely distressed? Perhaps you have already begun to see some important differences between the analytic and the cognitive-behavioural approaches, and may have begun to lean towards one or the other. If you have, ask yourself why. Is your inclination to do with your personality, or perhaps with avoidance? It is possible that we might choose, for example, psychodynamic counselling in order to put off having to make a decision, or a cognitive-behaviour therapy in order to avoid remembering childhood pain.

Among people we interviewed, we found that one had been asked to carry out tasks in an attempt to reduce her panic attacks; she reported that these had helped modestly, but that months later she was still having the attacks. On the other hand, someone who had been asked to practise self-management strategies at a particularly chaotic time in her life found them invaluable. If you feel that many of your problems stem from the past, and that help is to be found in memories and lengthy, detailed exploration of your emotional life, and if you prefer to talk and think about things instead of taking immediate action, then behaviour therapy probably is not for you. However, if you suffer from any phobia, specific anxiety, or obsessive-compulsive disorder that is result-ing in a wretched life, you may have a greater chance of real change through behaviour therapy.

The humanistic approaches

Humanistic approaches include Gestalt therapy, person-centred therapy, psychodrama, bio-energetics, primal therapy, and encounter groups. Some might also include existential therapy, transactional analysis (TA), and feminist therapy under this heading, as well as a whole host of the 'body work' approaches. Humanistic psychology is concerned with a holistic vision of human beings. There is an emphasis on personal experience and growth, awareness, human potential, health, feelings, spont-aneity and trust in one's body. Humanistic psychology and therapy is newer than psychoanalysis and behaviourism, and is to some extent associated perhaps with the idealism of the 1960s.

Generally, the humanistic approaches differ from the psycho-analytic in placing less emphasis on psychological conflict and sickness, less trust in 'experts' like psychoanalysts and behaviour therapists and intellectual theories, and more on trusting feelings and our bodies. Humanistic approaches are often more closely linked with spirituality than are psychoanalysis and behaviourism. The ethos of humanistic therapy is egalitarian and this is especially so in person-centred counselling, which is based on a refusal to believe that the therapist knows better, or that he or she should enact a role.

Carl Rogers probably deserves a paragraph to himself because he developed person-centred therapy somewhat independently and in opposition to both the psychoanalytic and behavioural schools. Person-centred counselling evolved from a close study of how people were actually helped. Rogers avoided formulating premature theories, and resisted the idea that he could interpret people's behaviour for them. Person-centred counselling rests on a kind of faith in innate human goodness and 'growthfulness'. It eschews false scientific conclusions and fashionable therapeutic techniques. Like other approaches, however, it has its critics.

One of the founding fathers of the humanistic movement, Wilhelm Reich showed how it is possible to discover how our bodies tense chronically against social demands, leading to psychosomatic illness and sexual problems, for example. In therapy, however, we can learn to trust our true instincts once more – to become self-actualizing. Participation in encounter groups, for example, encourages us to experiment with new or forgotten ways of being. People allow themselves to cry if they feel the need; to express anger fully; to know and express joy and love. In Gestalt therapy, on the other hand, you might be encouraged to bring your feelings into the present by talking *to* your mother, for example, as if she were in the room, sitting in the chair or on the floor cushion opposite you, instead of talking *about* her. Intellectualization would be discouraged because it allows you to conceal your true feelings. You may be encouraged to act out various scenes from your past or present, because by getting in touch with yourself in the here and now, it is possible to realize that holistic health is found in letting go and in trusting your instincts.

Humanistic therapy often borders on or resembles mystical practices; sometimes people will have 'peak experiences', when they transcend their everyday level of awareness. It is also possible to re-enact spontaneously with your entire body what happened in early childhood, babyhood, even birth and beyond. Imagery, song, dance, massage, and other forms of expression may be used, although practices vary from one school of humanistic therapy to another, some being quite sober, others wild and uninhibited.

Rachel, a librarian in her 30s, decided she needed to find out why it was so hard for her to express feelings of anger and tenderness. She chose to see a therapist who used a mixture of Gestalt, primal, and rebirthing techniques. She found within 18 months that she had grown up being 'good' for her parents, who had wanted 'a quiet life'. In therapy, she grieved for the years in which she had suppressed her own emotional life. She learned to trust her instincts, to experiment more, and to dress and express herself differently.

Humanistic therapies are probably unlikely to be found or offered in the NHS or other conventional institutions. Person-centred counselling is practised widely in student counselling services, where you will also find some Gestalt therapy in evidence. Most humanistic therapy, however, is practised in personal-growth centres, or in the homes and group practices of independent practitioners.

Behaviour therapists may suggest that humanistic practices are unscientific and undisciplined, and that they perhaps bear little resemblance to therapy at all. It differs from the psychoanalytic therapies in being usually much more expressive; clients will more often cry, laugh, shout, move around the room, lie on the floor, punch a cushion, or hug the therapist. Some comment that it seems more like a dramatic experience than a purposeful form of therapy; some suggest that it promotes temporary relief, but does not facilitate the full 'working through' that is believed to be necessary.

Who is likely to benefit from a humanistic approach? Again, note your own reactions: perhaps there is an immediate appeal in finally letting it all out, no longer holding back your real feelings, getting in touch with a kind of bodily energy, and sharing a social vision that perhaps many others seek. Perhaps you warm to the image of genuineness on offer in person-centred counselling or with the theatrical opportunities offered by Gestalt therapy and psychodrama.

If so, humanistic therapy may be an appropriate route for you. But think too whether its appeal may be founded on the idea of rebelling, and on getting quick, physical results (which it does not always). Perhaps it is all too easy for you to cry and shout, and to avoid a disciplined look at yourself, or a more committed approach to change that requires effort. As well, if you are seriously depressed or in any way emotionally fragile, humanistic therapy may be dangerous for you. There have been cases of people being pushed too hard to express their feelings. For example, one of our interviewees reported that he had been strongly encouraged by his therapist to feel certain 'baby feelings', with the result that he often left sessions in a confused state of mind and began to get panic attacks. He was eventually told by the therapist that it had gone beyond anything the therapist had handled before. Although there is an egalitarian ethos generally among humanistic practitioners, it has also been said that some have dangerous therapeutic ambitions, belonging to the dangerous, charismatic-guru category.

Transpersonal approaches

These are characterized by an interest in spirituality, mysticism, meditation, psychological astrology, and various paranormal or transcendental experiences. They are usually regarded by their proponents as representing a higher stage of evolution, that is, that those who have fewer neurotic problems – or who have 'done a lot of work on themselves' – have increased access to a higher realm of experience. Transpersonal therapy is sometimes though not necessarily aligned with an older age group. Jung, for example, often pointed out that the second half of life was as significant as youth and childhood.

We will not go into this approach very deeply here because we believe that most people who are looking for counselling or therapy probably need the sort of help offered by mainstream approaches. Occasionally people in therapy may have extra-ordinary experiences, such as reliving birth trauma or leaving their body. While some say that this sort of experience is highly significant, others say it is incidental and not necessarily a healing phenomenon at all. While many people claim to have all sorts of religious experiences and visions in transpersonal therapy, some of these are in fact expressions of psychotic illness. A warning attached to this approach, then, is not to confuse the extra-ordinary visions and experiences of some psychiatric illness with the genuinely transcendental.

Critics of these approaches suggest that people may be attracted to them for unhealthy reasons, for example, liking to think of themselves as special or as having extraordinary powers and perceptions; others simply state that this is not therapy at all, but a form of religion or entertainment. If you are involved in, or seek to become involved in, this type of therapy, make sure you ask yourself what your motives really are.

Transactional analysis (TA)

TA is enormously popular, probably due to the success of the bestselling *I'm OK, You're OK* by Thomas Harris. TA aims to do justice to both our current functioning and the childhood experiences and patterns underlying it. Its basic schema of ego states – the well-known Parent, Adult, and Child – has great appeal for many people since it offers a readily understandable picture of how we frequently react to others as if we are, for example, a carefree or intimidated child, a caring or authoritarian parent, or a more balanced adult. Over the years the theory and practice of TA has become very much more complex than this, but it has retained to some extent the original aim of explaining our psychological reactions in terms that are understandable to everyone. We suggest that you consult Kovel (1978) and Dryden (1994) for discussion of some of these other approaches.

In this brief survey of major therapeutic orientations we have obviously omitted dozens of particular approaches but hope that these sketches help to guide you. An appendix is included in order to help you calculate what may be the best approach for your current concerns.

Different therapeutic arenas

As we have pointed out, in addition to individual counselling or therapy, there are the 'arenas' of couple, family, and group counselling or therapy. Each of these has its own variety of training courses, institutes, and professional bodies. In each you will find some of the same multiplicity of theoretical orientations that we have just outlined: psychodynamic, person-centred, and behavioural, as well as other approaches unique to couple counselling.

In family therapy there are the approaches known as structural family therapy, strategic therapy, behavioural family therapy, and many others. In group therapy there is sensitivity training, encounter, psychodrama, group analytic therapy, cognitive-behavioural group therapy, and many others.

We briefly outline below some indications for the best use of each arena.

Individual counselling

Individual counselling and therapy are by far the most commonly practised, reflecting perhaps a preference for the individual attention and privacy they provide. The one-to-one format of client and counsellor does afford the highest level of undivided personal attention, privacy, and confidentiality. If you have extensive private worries or complex inner problems to discuss and if you are highly sensitive and need time to build a trusting relationship, this is probably the best arena for you. In a one-to- one situation the time is totally yours, unlike in a group, where you have to share time with other members as well as the counsellor's attention. This arena might not be best for you if you are inclined to become quickly, deeply, or intractably dependent on your counsellor. If you are adept at playing games and manipulating another person, again it might be best to avoid this arena, except with a very skilled counsellor. If you feel too threatened by – or, alternatively, too comfortable with – one-to-one intimacy to benefit from it, think twice. If your problems are primarily with a partner or family members, consider other arenas.

Couple counselling

This is also known as marital counselling or therapy; the use of the term 'couple' simply acknowledges the fact that we live in a changing society where heterosexual marriage is not necessarily the norm for a growing number of people.

If your problems are mainly concerned with an intimate partnership, usually couple counselling is indicated. Here, the relationship itself is the focus of the counselling, even when examining in some detail aspects of one person's thoughts or feelings. Individuals are sometimes seen separately for couple counselling, but the emphasis is on understanding, repairing – or dissolving – the relationship.

Couple counselling is not possible for those whose conflicts are so severe that they cannot sit in the same room together without violence or interminable arguing. It is unlikely to help when the source of difficulty stems mainly from one partner, for example, in the case of a mental illness. It also will not be highly effective if only one partner is committed to the process.

Family therapy

When one family member is identified by the family as having all the problems, or the most severe problems, yet it is recognized that the entire family has difficulties, family therapy is often indicated. Family therapists view the member with the problems as the symptom of family troubles, and regard the family in its entirety as the client. Relationships between all family members are observed, with the family all present. Issues of power, manipulation, and abuse are worked with. Sometimes family secrets, for example, sexual abuse, may be unearthed during therapy. Eating disorders, disruptive school behaviour, and bereavement are all sometimes treated in family therapy.

Family therapy cannot proceed without all, or most, members agreeing to attend and at least attempting to collaborate. Families unable to meet and interact with a minimal degree of control may not be able to receive help. Families which may include vulnerable members such as defenceless children or battered women may not benefit because of inherent risks. (See Howe, [1989] for clients' views of family therapy.)

Group therapy

There are many kinds of group therapy, but all offer the opportunity for strangers to observe each other's behaviour, hear each other's views and stories, and share feelings and problems. Many drug and alcohol rehabilitation programmes use groups extensively.

Some people feel safer in groups than in one-to-one counselling; some benefit from hearing others voice their pain and mistakes; and some are usefully denied access to manipulable one-to-one situations.

Groups offer a valuable chance to practise social skills and new behaviour before adopting them in real life. They also provide a means of studying styles of relating, or not, and the dynamics of group life.

Group therapy may be particularly threatening for highly

sensitive, disturbed, or paranoid individuals. It provides the least protection in terms of privacy and confidentiality; it also allows less time for individual attention than does one-to-one counselling.

Sometimes a natural progression occurs from individual to group therapy, particularly when someone is, for example, undergoing TA or primal therapy where part of the standard procedure is to combine individual and group approaches. Sometimes exposure to others can trigger off feelings and issues that had become stuck in individual work. Sometimes people attend individual counselling for their own needs, and also attend couple counselling when their relationship is in difficulties. It is inadvisable to try several arenas at the same time just as it is inadvisable to see two or more therapists at the same time. Rather than speeding things up, it will cause confusion, especially around divided loyalties and commitments. It is always worth considering, however, whether one type of therapy would be better than another, or in addition to these (group and individual; couple and individual, etc.)

Specialist and complementary treatments
If your main problems are sexual you might consider getting help from a sex therapist. Therapeutic methods range from the psychodynamic to the behavioural, in some cases involving learning actual techniques, for example, delaying ejaculation or enjoying penetration. Sometimes, for people who simply have no sexual knowledge or skill, it teaches them about sexual intercourse.

Sexual problems, smoking, nail-biting, insomnia, obesity, and phobias make up a group of problems that are often targeted by hypnotherapists. Many people are attracted to hypnotherapy in the belief that the therapist has all the answers and can 'magic' away the problems. Hypnotherapy is not as mysterious or magical as its popular image suggests, and relies on the principle of deep relaxation and the encouragement of existing personal strengths. It does not cure psychological problems but helps to remove symptoms, sometimes very successfully. Caution should be exercised by people who think they may have serious underlying problems.

Art therapy, dramatherapy, dance and movement therapy, aromatherapy, massage, reflexology, homeopathy, and many other approaches also claim to address and resolve psychological problems. Some are regulated to some extent by their own professional bodies, and some by statutory bodies. If any of these appeals to you, investigate them, but use similar criteria to evaluate whether they can help you as those we are recommending throughout this book. There is one point that we cannot stress enough. *If you have any severe disorders you should always consult your doctor first.* We know that some people do not trust the Establishment and its doctors and medicines, but you may be at risk if you avoid proper assessment and help and opt for alternative or complementary medicine. If you decide to try this route, do check credentials and methods with reputable professional bodies first.

Short-term or long-term?

Some approaches stress short-term and some long-term therapy. There is also long-term counselling and short-term psychotherapy. It is more helpful if you consider your views on the options without being swayed by the names. Critics of brief (short-term) therapy say it cheats people of the opportunity to really explore themselves in depth; it is sometimes portrayed as an economic shortcut. Long-term therapy, however, is criticized as encouraging dependency and passivity, and discouraging problem-solving and therapeutic activity.

Those who have researched and developed forms of brief treatment have great professional integrity, and have devised many challenging methods – for example, cognitive-analytic therapy; the two-plus-one model; single-session therapy; and intensive, short-term dynamic psychotherapy. These are not truncated forms of long-term therapy, and are not designed to deprive you of the full help you need. Many people need and prefer short-term approaches. Where there is a need or preference for long-term therapy, as far as possible it should be provided, although there is obviously a limit to the length of therapy that is available through the public sector.

There is today a growing desire to bring different therapies together under a common rationale and language. If a widely agreed explanation for psychological problems could be found among professionals, then counselling and psychotherapy would be more credible and more understandable to the public. However, such are the historical and philosophical differences between the many schools, that many are pessimistic about the prospects

Eclecticism is a pragmatic endeavour of many practitioners who aim to use the most promising therapeutic elements from the many approaches. Some pioneers have developed forms of eclecticism which seek to deliver to clients a systematic assessment of what they need and the therapy to accompany it. Multi-modal therapy, for example, aims to discover each client's background, specific problems, contributory factors, ways of experiencing life and its problems, best fit with therapists, and so on.

In the current state of the therapeutic arts, we believe in the realities of time and money, the needs of many distressed individuals, and current research results, which add up to promising developments in models of time-sensitive counselling and systematically eclectic therapy. Once again, however, we caution you against throwing yourself into the latest therapeutic fad: the world of counselling and psychotherapy is littered with discarded enthusiasms.

7
What Happens in the Course of Your Therapy or Counselling?

Although what happens in therapy and counselling differs from person to person, there are typical issues which emerge. Some therapists think in terms of a beginning, middle, and ending phase of therapy, and there is no reason why you should not as well. Below we consider what the typical features of these phases may be, bearing in mind that we are making very broad generalizations that may well not always apply to the individual client.

The beginning phase

If you are completely new to counselling you may be full of ideas, fantasies, hopes, anxieties, and feelings both during your sessions and in between If there is no one in your personal life who listens closely to you, then you will have the 'strange' experience of someone giving you their exclusive attention for an hour (or more) a week. They will listen with interest, without judgement, and responsively; they will not, as in everyday conversations, interrupt you to tell you about their experiences.

Some counsellors from the very beginning engage in absolutely minimal small-talk, explanatory conversation, assessment, and contracting. You may find yourself walking into a stranger's house, into a strange room, being ushered to a chair, and being asked something as simple as, 'What can I do for you?', or, 'Where would you like to begin?' If you are in a crisis or acute distress, you may feel a need simply to launch into your story, starting anywhere and filling in the details as you go; you may want to sink into the chair and weep. More typically, if this is your first time you will probably ask, 'Where do I begin?' While there is no correct place to begin your explanation of why you have come for counselling, if you are attending a statutory clinic or short-term facility, or if your counsellor has a goal-oriented approach such as cognitive-behavioural counselling, you will be encouraged to begin focusing on your most pertinent issues fairly promptly. Generally speaking, humanistic and psychodynamic practitioners may require altogether less focus. You have the right to decide either that you need to 'get right down to business' or to spill out your feelings, or to take your time to get used to the setting and to settle into a pace that suits you.

It may feel as if it is impossible to find a suitable place to begin. Remembering that you probably have several or many sessions ahead of you, means you need not worry about explaining everything in this first session. If you feel overwhelmed by negative and confused feelings, your therapist will probably help you to find a starting point. One way of finding a focus is to try to settle on a single word or phrase that roughly describes your predicament or your predominant feelings or thoughts. It may be 'depressed', 'confused', 'hopeless', 'needy', 'weird', or anything; it is your word, it is a beginning, and you are not being 'diagnosed' by using it. Or it may be a phrase like, 'Everything in my life is just screwed up', or, 'I just keep thinking it's too late for me.' Alternatively, you may be the kind of person who feels things physically or thinks in pictures: 'I just ache with the loss of him', or, 'I keep seeing myself as old, alone, and unwanted', may be the kinds of descriptions that come to mind.

New clients sometimes go blank and may say something like, 'I don't know why I've come, really. When I called you I felt bad, but now I feel fine.' Or, 'Perhaps I'm here on false pretences; I expect you see a lot of people who are more deserving of help than me.' These kinds of statements usually reveal a lot about how you see yourself (as unworthy, for example) and may form the basis for analysing your self-image. Some therapists may focus on such sentences immediately; others will simply encourage you to settle in and use the session for whatever is important to *you*.

It can be frightening to have someone finally take you seriously – it is not surprising, then, that you may dry up, feel like a fraud, and wonder if you are wasting the therapist's and your time. Generally, people get through this initial obstacle relatively easily and begin talking about bits of their life story, their current circumstances and the particular aspects of their lives in which they feel unhappy or confused.

From the outset you and your counsellor will be noticing each other's reactions and weighing them up. You may be in awe of the counsellor or unsure of their ability to understand you. You may even wish to shut the counsellor out of your awareness and talk at the floor, as it were. Likewise your counsellor will initially be trying to get the measure of you, adjusting his or her listening, expectations, and reactions in order to tune into you. The interaction between you may feel relaxed and full of rapport, or uneasy and awkward.

Most counsellors and therapists will probably spend some time during the first session or sessions getting information from you, helping you to decide on your objectives in coming to therapy, and making some form of contract or agreement. People often feel rather passive in this process, perhaps because expertise is attributed to the therapist, or perhaps because they are not on their home ground.

Earlier chapters have discussed the kinds of problems brought to counsellors; what basic expectations you may have; and what you should be prepared to ask. All such preparation, however, will not necessarily equip you to deal with your feelings when you arrive for your first session, nor the counsellor's own agenda and personality. If the counsellor dislikes extensive contracting, assessment, and goal-setting, for example, you may abandon your questions and go along with the counsellor's way of doing things. Ideally, you should feel able to ask the questions you want to ask, regardless of the counsellor's 'style'.

Let us suppose, instead, that there is a certain amount of discussion about ethical and practical agreements, about your preference for setting goals, or for simply talking in order to 'see what comes up'. At this point you and your counsellor have some agreements as to how you are both working – you have a baseline to which you can refer later and against which you can measure progress. In briefer, focused counselling, your goals will be attended to and actively worked on from the very beginning. In open-ended and long-term counselling or therapy you may at times meander in your discussion, perhaps returning again and again to certain key issues. Depending on the kind of approach, your counselling may be mainly an intense, cathartic experience, about which you think deeply between sessions, or it may have a structured agenda, including clear goals, homework assignments, vigorous challenging, and risk-taking. If you are recently bereaved, for example, you may experience great relief from counselling, whereas if you are concerned with overcoming social anxieties, you may be involved in practising new behaviour between sessions.

In this beginning phase you will become aware of whether you wish to commit yourself to a lengthy process of a year or more of therapy, to a period of some months, or, rather, to a few weeks. Many therapists have their own preferences and some will not agree to begin work with you unless your basic commitment is to a long-term process. Many therapists suggest an initial meeting in which you can judge whether you would like to continue with the therapist, perhaps followed by four or six further sessions, which will be followed by further agreements as to the time commitment. If you are feeling ambivalent about what you are getting into, it may be a temptation to leave prematurely; at this stage you would do well to remember that committing yourself to a few more sessions can pay dividends.

During this phase you may experience strong feelings about the therapist. You may feel a powerful sense of love, that this is the most caring person in the universe, and so on. You may try to please your therapist by using their vocabulary. In certain approaches these phenomena are seen as part of the therapeutic process, in others they may be seen as obstacles to the real focus of therapeutic work. Many clients find their therapy going awry at this point, paying an inordinate amount of attention to the person of the therapist instead of sticking to their original agenda.

Overall, the beginning may feel exciting, frightening, helpful in the relief that it brings, and reassuring. You may feel wonderful, or, more modestly, a little more hopeful. Perhaps you already suspect, however, that it is not going to be all fun and plain-sailing from now on, that counselling or therapy is not magic, but more like relentless soul-searching and hard work. You may begin the process by talking a great deal about external events and other people, and seeing yourself and your life choices in somewhat fixed terms.

The middle phase

There is no precise point at which a middle stage begins. It may happen after weeks, months, or even years; it may even happen with a different therapist or counsellor. In this period there is a sense that your initial worries and fantasies about counselling have mellowed, and the novelty has probably worn off. You may have achieved certain goals – such as standing up for yourself a little more, feeling less depressed, or being able to speak to strangers – or your goals may have changed. What brought you to counselling may turn out to have been only the tip of an iceberg: perhaps you were feeling stressed, or wanted to talk about a career change, and begin to realize that you have been anxious for years, that you hate your career, or that you have never come to terms with your father's death.

Josie spent the first few sessions in therapy getting to know and trust her therapist. She talked about the problems connected with her upbringing in children's homes. This was a subject she had talked about often with friends, but mostly with a sense of aimless anger and resentment. With her therapist, Josie began to understand the inevitability of her past, and the strengths she had developed because of and in spite of it. She began to accept that effort for changing her future was in her hands. In other words, her negativity gradually changed into new understanding and responsibility.

Jonathan thought his counsellor was wonderful when he met her. After each of his first few sessions, he would leave feeling ten feet tall, having expressed things he had kept inside himself for years, and having felt really listened to for the first time. He told his friends what a marvellous thing counselling was. Two months later, however, Jonathan's euphoria wore off; the counsellor began to appear more ordinary, less ideal, and more like someone he felt obliged to see, rather than he wanted to see. It took him great effort to realize that he was getting in touch with many disappointed and frustrated feelings based in the past, which he eventually came to understand. His middle phase was characterized by a crisis of confidence.

Exactly what happens for *you* in this phase depends on many different things. You may have complete trust in your counsellor, or you may resist his or her efforts to help you. You may feel somewhat raw emotionally as parts of your personality are exposed in a way you are not used to. Or this may be a time of confrontation for you: 'Do I really want to change all that much, considering the hard work involved? Or am I content with the way I am now?' Therapy may be especially challenging in the middle phase, as certain home truths are brought to our attention and relentlessly focused on over and over again. The temptation to 'escape' from therapy – and the truth – may be strong at such points.

If your experience of counselling is that an acute distress or difficulty has been rapidly relieved (say, your panic attacks), you may decide that is enough for you. But the reduction in your panic attacks may coincide with a realization that you are not so happy in other areas of your life, or recall how you were frequently left alone by your parents. New discoveries that emerge within your counselling sessions may convince you that you need to commit yourself to more than you had originally intended.

In this phase, you might feel freer to ask questions. For example, if your session is at 8 o'clock in the evening and you notice the counsellor yawning, you may ask, 'Are you tired?' Perhaps you are genuinely concerned about his or her welfare. The same question, however, could mean, 'Are you really paying attention to me? Am I the last in a long line of clients today? Are you trying to squeeze too many clients in, and am I getting the service I should be getting?' These are fair questions. On seeing your counsellor yawning you might ask 'Are you bored?' This question can signify that you are really concerned that you may be boring – or it could be a sarcastic challenge. Sometimes people ask questions instead of making statements. Hence, instead of saying, 'I'm fed up seeing you yawn in our sessions', you may hide your anger and disguise it as a quasi-legitimate question.

As the session nears its end, another typical question is, 'Is the time nearly up?' If you have no watch on, this may be simply a request for information, but it is often an expression of anxiety. Something painful may have been touched on during the session and you can't wait to get out of the room and try to escape from the pain. Alternatively, people sometimes ask this question as a prelude to making a new and risky disclosure. If you time such a disclosure carefully, you may just about blurt it out leaving no further time for discussion, and again you can make your escape! Counsellors tend to be alert to the nuances of such manoeuvres, and it can often be more beneficial if you learn to take the risk of making such disclosures earlier on in sessions, so that they can be fully explored.

Then there are questions which may be categorized as testing the boundaries, as being manipulative, intrusive, flirtatious, and so on. 'Can we go out for dinner sometime?' could be a naive invitation intended on a purely friendly basis. What can some-times lie behind such questions, however, is that the client is pushing the limits, testing to see if they can win the counsellor over, and perhaps make themselves 'special'. Some people have been known to make such 'advances', perhaps unconsciously testing to see whether the counsellor really is trustworthy or 'just like all (bad) men/women'. Open flirtation is another matter. A question like, 'Do you think I'm attractive?' may be flirtatious but could also mean, 'I feel really bad about my appearance but I'm not sure how others see me', or, 'My father never took any notice of me.' It could mean all sorts of things, and the counsellor's training predisposes him or her to be vigilant and thoughtful in regard to alternative and deeper meanings.

Certain questions may be asked simply as a way of filling in time, covering embarrassing silences, changing from a painful subject, expressing friendliness, or attempting to feel at ease. 'Where are you going on your holiday?'; 'Do you have children?'; and 'Have you lived here long?' are often questions of this kind. Some therapists will answer you directly, while some will make it plain from the outset that they will never answer personal questions about themselves. Sometimes questions like these may be simply 'nosiness', and even rudeness. 'How much money do you make?' is considered by a majority in our society to be a taboo question, for example. There is a fine line between undue inquisitiveness and rightful enquiry. 'Don't you think that black people are discriminated against?' is a perfectly justified question for you to ask, but what if your counsellor's response were, 'Yes I do, sometimes, but not invariably'? If you expect 100 per cent agreement and this is important to you, you would either become involved in a political argument with the therapist, or decide not to return next time.

Remember that one of the overriding aims of all counselling and psychotherapy is to help you discover your full potential or your adult self, or to build your confidence. Taking the risk of asking questions can be a valuable part of this. To ask 'Do you think I'm attractive?', for example, may sometimes be part of a flirtatious game, but it could also be a highly vulnerable thing to ask. What if your therapist were to say, 'No, I don't actually'? Even if she or he were not to reply at all, asking such a question can have immense power for you. It can mean that you are putting all your doubts about yourself on the line.

One of the opportunities afforded to you by the therapeutic situation is that you can experiment freely. Perhaps if you can risk asking new questions, and survive, you can learn to ask the kinds of questions you want to in 'real life'. In other words, you can practise useful social and interpersonal skills in therapy, and often in the middle phase these skills include asking questions, negotiating, clarifying, complaining and being assertive. In our view, good counsellors should encourage you to do just this.

Another phenomenon in this phase is the identification of patterns of behaviour, thinking, and feeling. As you disclose your memories, stories, anecdotes, aspirations, and examples of typical everyday behaviour, your counsellor will be building a comprehensive picture of you. You may then be helped to see – or you may see for yourself – for example, the kinds of self-defeating thoughts you have, the 'games' you play, the recurring interpersonal difficulties you get yourself into. You may also come to see connections between the roots of these patterns – the past – and their occurrence in your present life. Approaches such as transactional analysis, cognitive-analytic therapy, and psychodynamic counselling often highlight such patterns and their possible origins.

One of the major attributes of counselling and psychotherapy is the opportunity you are given to bring together the various pieces of your life, and to look at these in order to make some overall sense. What at first appears to be an unfortunate crisis may, with therapeutic help, become understandable as part of a pattern, and then the source and cause of this pattern. Sometimes by seeing that we are needlessly repeating behaviour patterns which no longer serve us well we are released from their 'spell'. Sometimes the 'seeing' is not enough, and we must work hard to overcome our patterns and to replace them with more productive behaviour.

By using the there-and-then and the here-and-now, a rhythm of reflection and interpretation may be established, allowing you and your counsellor to examine past and present alternately, or to concentrate on one or the other as necessary. It is part of the therapist's skill and job to observe and point out to you when you avoid paying attention to painful or especially challenging areas of your behaviour; the successful workaholic may be trying to avoid his or her painful past by filling up the present, while someone who talks interminably about their childhood may be trying to avoid taking action to change an empty life in the present.

While your counsellor or therapist is listening, observing, interpreting, challenging, and helping you to stay 'on course', what is your role?

Increasingly throughout therapy you will have to come to terms with your own responsibility. You can talk about things in therapy forevermore, as if you are talking about another person. You can listen to your therapist's perceptive and timely remarks without actually taking them in or acting on them. There has to come a time when the talking has a real impact, when it 'bites' and incites one to action. Perhaps you began therapy thinking it is a magical or mysterious process that unfolds effortlessly, guided by the therapist's unerring hand. As time goes by, however, you will not be able to avoid the awareness that this is not the case. What is talked about is *you*, and any changes you wish to make in your life have to be initiated by *you*. Gradually, you come to realize that although you may often feel like a helpless, timid child, you are in fact an adult with sole responsibility for your own life decisions.

Carl Rogers suggested that when people begin counselling, many of them see themselves in rigid terms, as trapped in circumstances, for example. As counselling proceeds, there is often a typical movement to seeing themselves as potent agents with real choices in their lives. The American psychotherapist Arnold Lazarus observed that on starting therapy many people at first distance themselves from the therapist by discussing external, factual subjects, or by talking about their troubles in highly self-censoring ways. Although a certain stiffness or personal distance may be inevitable for most first-time clients, you may find it helps to get into the real 'meat' of your concerns, and, hence, closer to getting better, sooner. This is shown in Lazarus' diagram (Figure 1).

Zone E represents your superficial contact with the world, for example, talking to your banker. **Zone D** represents your relationships with slight acquaintances, which is characterized by social niceties and small talk. In **Zone C** we find your relationships with your widest circle of friends and family members which, although cordial and familiar, are limited in intimacy and trust. **Zone B** represents your closest friends, those in whom you readily confide. **Zone A** is filled with your most private,

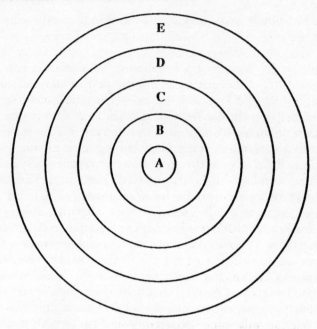

Figure 1 Your inner and outer zones.

innermost, and sensitive thoughts, feelings, memories, fantasies, and secrets. Psychoanalysts would add a perhaps deeper and more protected zone which contains material that is kept even from ourselves until the time is right to know it.

To help you most effectively, your therapist ideally needs to make contact with your inner zones. By the time you have worked through the beginning phase of therapy, you will probably have shed your most obvious reservations and resistances. Any social rigidity should have worn off, and you will be ready to allow your therapist to see the real you. Therapists cannot, however, force you to reveal more than you wish to. Clients may in this phase move from Zone D to C and B, with occasional forays into Zone A. For some people it is a simple matter to concentrate almost entirely on material in Zone A, but for others it is a frightening journey. Our innermost concerns and fears can include all sorts of fantasies. Deep down, perhaps you feel like a complete fraud or an empty and uninteresting person; perhaps beneath the mask of the 'macho' manager you are a terrified child; or beneath the persona of the angry anarchist you may be a bourgeois romantic, longing for a cosy existence. Deep down, I may secretly harbour the idea that I am not like other people at all – I am hideous or special. I may have a secret, terrible suspicion that I am insane, or diseased, or doomed to an utterly miserable life. I may have sexual fantasies of an outlandish, even criminal nature. Whatever is most secret, personal and precious is guarded. The question you will be asking yourself may be, 'Will I let the therapist in? Will my therapist be able to help me explain this thing, and will he or she be able to accept it when it is out in the open?'

Depth and risk, then, are features of this phase. Sometimes when there are such worries or intimations of bigger problems inside us, we are faced with the dilemma of whether to go on, take a risk, or sink inside ourselves. Many of the long silences in some therapies, and periods characterized by stubborn impasses, may be attributable to such dilemmas. Therapists are optimistic, and sometimes idealistic, and may encourage you to stay when you wish to leave, or to broaden your goal when you wish to stick to your original, perhaps modest agenda. There may, therefore, be a struggle at this time between your aspirations and your therapist's. We look at this further in Chapter 9.

Counselling and therapy may become difficult for you at this time: you thought you would just talk about your public-speaking anxiety for a couple of sessions and here you are, a year later, getting into deep emotional water. Or maybe you thought counselling would be a methodical, progressive affair – and instead find there are many false starts, unproductive sessions, and frequently a sense of taking one step forward and two back. Sometimes going to a session feels like a pointless empty ritual, and indeed it may be, but how can you tell? (Chapters 8 and 9 will help you here.) Or perhaps you have never felt so pleased with yourself, so much in touch with your 'real self' – yet friends tell you that you have changed, and you sense they may not like you this way. Even though you can talk about these things to your counsellor, you are still alone in your life decisions.

The ending phase

If your aim in going for counselling was to manage your stress, sleep better, or be able to travel on airplanes and you have achieved these aims, then perhaps that is the end of the matter.

Your counsellor has been an effective helper – a professional who has helped you in return for some form of payment, like any other professional. You had a contract, you got what you wanted; there was no mystery involved.

More usually, however, things do not always work out quite so smoothly. Your goals may vary over the course of counselling, and you may establish a close relationship with your counsellor which has become meaningful, and not lightly ended.

Many counsellors and therapists help their clients to separate from therapy by increasing homework assignments and self-therapy, and having fewer sessions. In time-limited therapy there is always an end in sight, which enables you to prepare yourself. Most therapy, however, is open-ended: it is up to you and your therapist to decide when the time is right to end.

Psychodynamic counsellors, and others who emphasize the importance of the relationship between client and counsellor, regard the ending phase as highly significant because it may echo earlier endings and separations. If you have a good ending with your counsellor, which usually involves letting yourself feel the pain and sadness of parting, then earlier emotional hurts may be healed or put into perspective. For these reasons some counsellors like to make a contract for ending. You may be discouraged from ending suddenly, and asked instead to attend further sessions in order to deal with the ending. There are differences of opinion about this. One ex-client told us she could see no point in the last few sessions, but she went through with it just to keep the counsellor happy – at the same time resenting having to pay. Others, however, value such an ending. Our own view is that it is entirely up to you.

At the end of your counselling or therapy, you may want to give your counsellor a gift, write them a letter, or hug them. Some will welcome such expressions of gratitude, others will encourage you to verbalize your feelings instead. You may be invited to call again any time in the future, or you may be encouraged to regard your therapy as absolutely ended. Sometimes you will be offered a follow-up session, which gives both of you the chance to review matters with hindsight.

Most counsellors and therapists decline any invitations to become friends after the therapy is over, although this does sometimes happen. Most therapists feel very strongly that there should be no sexual contact whatsoever between client and therapist, during or after the ending of therapy.

In therapy and counselling there are few guarantees, some setbacks and misunderstandings, and usually a degree of disappointment. It may be normal and healthy to experience disappointment because this is more in line with reality – life is not everything we would like it to be. There are people who claim to have derived amazing benefits from therapy and counselling, and who testify that it radically transformed or saved their lives. Equally, there are some who claim to have been abused, or that they have been cheated, and have wasted money and time. We look at success and failure in therapy and counselling – and how to know what is happening to *you* – in the following two chapters.

8
How Do You Know When Your Counselling is Succeeding?

It may seem obvious that if you feel better during the course of your therapy or counselling, then it must be succeeding. Unfortunately, it is not so obvious. Consider the person who feels immensely relieved to find a therapist to talk to and who immediately 'feels better'. Soon after therapy has ended, however, he or she rapidly begins to feel worse. Or the person who quickly *feels* better but continues to make a mess of his or her life. It is a fairly typical experience for a client to have been in counselling for some time, but not to be sure whether they are getting better. The sense of progress and of well-being is often highly subjective. Your therapist may tell you that you have changed, yet you may not feel any different from when you started. Your therapist may tell you that progress is slow, and you may not appreciate how successful the therapy is until some time in the future; he or she may even suggest that your preoccupation with measuring the success of your therapy is an obstacle – as it may be if you do not give it a fair chance to work.

It is not so easy, then, to tell when counselling or therapy is succeeding. One way of understanding what a successful therapeutic experience constitutes is to consider a model of therapy based on shared goals, tasks, and bonds.

Goals

If you were not clear on entering therapy what your aims were, you will have little to look back on to measure your progress. Some of those we have spoken to about their unsuccessful experiences of counselling and therapy were not clear about their goals. One man admitted that he had felt he 'should' have some therapy because he was in a caring profession and many of his colleagues were 'in therapy'. If your unadmitted goal is to fit in with others or to be fashionable, then you will probably find your therapy dissatisfying. An astute therapist, however, should be able to help you to identify that your initial motives and goals are unclear.

We recommend that you make some notes or keep a record of your worries and problems *before* starting counselling. It is also a good idea to write down some clear ideas about your specific goals. These may be in the form of, 'I want to feel less nervous around people', or, 'I would like to wake up feeling good about life.' These are very broad goals, but at least present you with yardsticks. 'I want to be more assertive at work'; 'I want to be able to have a close relationship', or 'I want to overcome my panic attacks' are more specific goals.

You and your therapist may discuss and agree on such goals at the initial contracting stage of your therapy. Sometimes your original goals are forgotten or abandoned, and you may be seduced by your own, and possibly your counsellor's, fascination with all sorts of other aspects of your life. If you have clear goals, you can remind yourself whether you are working towards them, or wandering off and avoiding them.

Many people like to keep a diary or journal of their reflections during counselling. By writing a few notes each week you will have an account of your progress to look back on. You may realize on reading back that you have come quite a long way. Some people, particularly if they are depressed, believe they will never improve, or that only total improvement is worthwhile. A diary can show in black and white the small but significant pieces of success that have occurred since counselling began.

You and your therapist may agree on a week-by-week assessment of progress, or possibly a fortnightly or monthly review. In some forms of time-limited therapy, for example cognitive-analytic therapy, it is common practice to construct a simple graph in order to measure success or failure (Appendix 2 shows how goals can be recorded and scored on a week-by-week basis). You should be aware that for many therapists this kind of exercise does not fit in with their approach. Nevertheless, there is nothing to prevent you from keeping your own progress chart.

Another way of 'measuring' your progress is to ask yourself a series of questions and to write your answers, possibly discussing them with your therapist. For example, you might ask:

- What are my goals in therapy?

- What am I prepared to do to achieve these?
- How will I know when I've achieved them?
- How can I prove my success?
- How might I reward myself for succeeding?
- What sort of time-span do I think is realistic for success?
- How might I sabotage my own goals?
- How might I deny that I've made progress when I really have?
- What will I learn from any lack of success?
- Could my counsellor and I discuss the possible reasons for failures?
- What further goals might I have after achieving my initial goals?

Sometimes you need some modest goals to aim at in the beginning, which will later take you in the direction of your more ambitious goals. For someone who is depressed, for example, an initial (small) goal may be simply to spend ten minutes a day doing something positive, with the eventual, 'bigger' aim of leading a fulfilled life. It can be helpful to present yourself with positive goals: 'I want to enjoy my life more' has a different quality from, 'I don't want to be depressed.' And you may find it more motivating: 'I want to be able to relate to people, to say what I'm feeling, and enjoy myself in company' has greater motivating power than, 'I don't want to be so lonely, inhibited, and unhappy.'

Tasks

It may seem that if you and your counsellor explicitly agree on goals, everything should proceed nicely. However, although you may both agree to work on, say, your tendency to avoid social situations, you may still have different agendas about how you are going to reach your goal of becoming more socially confident. Your assumption may be that your counsellor is going to set you certain behaviour-changing tasks, and your counsellor's assumption may be that you are going to spend some time looking in to your early childhood in search of the causes of your insecurity. Or you may assume that your counsellor wants to hear details of your fascinating dream life; he or she, however, wishes to help you to identify instances of your irrational thinking or avoidant behaviour. Even if you are aware of your counsellor's theoretical orientation, you may have different ideas about the ways in which it will be applied. Some clear discussion about the proposed tasks that are to be used in helping you towards your goals is likely to reduce misunderstandings, and lead to more effective counselling.

Clients often believe that change happens mysteriously or somewhat magically: place yourself in the counsellor's hands, talk about yourself, and everything just falls into place. This does not happen. Counselling skills, techniques, and strategies are used consciously by the counsellor. Even when your counsellor appears to be doing nothing but listening intently, they are probably also formulating thoughts, deciding when to intervene, what to say, and how best to help you to find your own solutions and insights. Certain 'tasks' are always involved, whether obvious or not. Counsellors cannot explain each and every utterance they make, but some will be quite ready to explain to you why they have asked or said something that you may not have immediately understood. Some may be rather cryptic or 'withholding'. The less clarity and agreement there is on all such tasks, the greater the likelihood that a rift will develop between you and your counsellor.

One of the signs that the counselling is succeeding is that your counsellor challenges you with tasks during and between sessions that have specific applications to your problems and concerns. A good counsellor will know what is necessary to reach you and stretch you. Sometimes these tasks involve doing specific things. You may be asked to look at old photographs of someone you have lost, to record your dreams, or to talk to strangers. Less obviously, and perhaps more frustratingly, you may simply be asked to say whatever comes into your mind. As long as you trust the counsellor's rationale for what he or she is doing, and you accept that it is relevant to your problems, it bodes well for success. If you are constantly mystified by what your counsellor says or does, and feel unable to ask what is happening, or to express your concern, then your counselling may be threatened.

Bonds

'I knew immediately I wasn't going to get on with this person', said one of our interviewees. In this case, the client had been allocated a therapist within a free service and had no choice about the therapist whom he found cold and critical. Although the client tried hard to make a success of it, the therapy failed.

Most of us instinctively know when we meet people with whom we feel things will go well. Being on the same wavelength sometimes happens immediately and sometimes slowly, but it is quite different from one of resistance and dislike. While we can learn from people we do not feel warmly towards, it is likely to require much more work. Rapport, warmth, and mutual liking all provide good grounding for successful therapy. Warmth and friendliness on the counsellor's part is deliberately disciplined and kept within the confines of the counselling room; do not mistake warmth for a sign that your counsellor wants to befriend you beyond the counselling setting.

If you are a shy or unsociable person, you may not wish to form a rapid, warm relationship with a therapist or counsellor. You might prefer, and need, to take a while to adjust to the intimacy of the therapeutic situation. You may prefer a therapist or style of therapy that is 'impersonal'. Some people like close relationships with their therapists in which they may hug them and cry with them; others dislike this. In your search for a therapist, take into account what the best possible match for you is in terms of warmth or coolness. Similarly, you may want to work with a clinician, someone you can relate to mainly at a professional level; alternatively, you might prefer an enthusiastic beginning practitioner. Sometimes the match between client and counsellor overrides questions of qualification or experience.

If you get on well with your counsellor and feel positively about the understanding between you, these are good omens. What else is important? You might think that if you feel better, trust your own feelings, that is all there is to it. While people often do feel better initially because they have found someone who gives them exclusive attention, how can you be sure this good feeling is real and durable? Suppose that you look forward tremendously to your sessions and admire your counsellor; you talk to your friends about counselling, adopt the jargon of counselling, and generally appear to have changed. For some people, entry into the world of therapy represents a sense of acceptance, and sometimes even an apparent 'rebirth' which can resemble religious conversion. Is this success? This sort of adoption of a new persona is often like a thin veneer, rather than signifying any real change or success. People may change the way they talk and dress, and even change jobs and relationships, but sometimes such changes substitute for real inner change. Signs of success in therapy include greater autonomy and a genuine sense of self, which does not necessarily have to be expressed in dramatic outward changes.

Varieties of success

If people in your life seem to relate to you more positively, and perhaps even spontaneously compliment you on how much brighter you seem, these are good signs. If you feel freer to relate to people, to try new behaviour, and enjoy ordinary everyday life more, these too are good signs. Such indicators of therapeutic success may not come overnight, so their absence does not mean your therapy is a failure. You may well have to go down – to become depressed or to grieve, for example – before you go up. Or you may experience therapy as a series of ups and downs. However, if you have had years of therapy and rarely, if ever, feel better, or receive comments that you are changing, think what this may mean. If the therapy is working, you are likely at some point to have more understanding of yourself, and to realize that more options lie before you than you had suspected. Therapy is a process of looking at yourself and your experience of life from new angles.

Unless counselling is to be an end in itself, you will find that you are actively involved in reflecting on yourself and experimenting with new ways of thinking, feeling, and behaving. One of the surest signs that counselling is working is that you become aware of taking inside yourself what you learn. Rather than sitting at the feet of the counsellor, lapping up their wisdom, you find you are stimulated to challenge yourself, to reconsider the limitations and distortions of your ways of thinking – you take on your therapist's role. You may respond differently to life situations, and sometimes to deliberately try out new behaviour, for example, 'I told my mother I didn't want to see her this Christmas; I was amazed I was able to do that', or, 'I walked into a café the other day on my own – I've never been able to do that.'

Some people report that as they become less preoccupied with their problems they are freer to enjoy simple, everyday feelings; for example, they notice flowers for the first time, or enjoy small talk with their neighbours. Such changes may be directly related to the client's goals and are by-products of therapy. On the other hand, some people have reported, for example, being free of headaches for the first time in years since having counselling, even though this was not an explicit aim.

Success in therapy may be paradoxical. For example, it may mean giving up certain parts of life that had previously been important: people sometimes leave partners when they realize they have been enmeshed in self-defeating, neurotic relationships; some leave lucrative careers, which they come to realize do not fulfil them emotionally. Clients will even say that although therapy may not have helped them to become any happier, it restored a sense of self-respect or a sense of ownership of their life for the first time in years. Clients may turn their backs on 'society', needing to spend time rediscovering nature, for example; others may give up a dream of communal living and become stockbrockers!

There is no guarantee that therapy will make you happy, creative, wise, rich, or healthy. Its main aim is to address your problems and aspirations in such a way that you will gain greater insight into yourself, and encounter fewer obstacles within. While counselling and therapy aim to restore self-determination, they cannot make you into a wholly new person; neither can your therapist make your life-decisions for you. You may consider counselling successful if you lose the illusion that everyone has a better life than you. In other words, getting in touch with unavoidable realities rather than spending your time day-dreaming, fantasizing, and moaning may be regarded as successful conclusions to therapy.

You will know if your therapy is succeeding if you are learning new ways of looking at yourself. You may be content to wait years, or you may prefer to be actively engaged in understanding your own thinking, feeling, and behaviour patterns. One of the great advantages of learning distinct ways of helping yourself is that you do not suddenly feel bereft when you terminate therapy. If your therapist helps you to learn and take in new ways of dealing with life, you become your own therapist. Consider the following example:

Michael was shy, unassertive and unambitious. He felt he was getting nowhere with his life; his girlfriend had left him, and his job was dull. Initial explorations in counselling revealed that he had come from a family in which everyone was somewhat shy. He had changed schools several times because his parents had had to move house often, and he had not been able to form enduring friendships; instead, he had become even more introverted. Michael came to expect not to make friends and therefore did not, a self-fulfilling prophecy. He was capable of a great deal more than he was achieving at work, but was too afraid to believe in himself or to assert himself, and therefore aimed low in his professional aspirations. Michael became involved in a vicious circle of demoralization, which resulted in his girlfriend finding him too miserable to endure.

Michael quickly agreed on this description of his problems. More specifically, he agreed to look closely at some of his typical thoughts and expectations. 'I've never been able to make friends, and I never will'; 'I haven't got what it takes'; 'I couldn't possibly strike up and continue a conversation myself' were some of his abiding beliefs. After some encouragement from his counsellor, Michael agreed that more realistic and helpful thoughts would include, 'I've had trouble making friends, but there's no reason I can't learn to do so'; 'Nothing dreadful will happen to me if I try to initiate conversations and they go wrong.' By working hard at these reconstructed thoughts and experimenting with them in real life (Michael deliberately struck up conversations with strangers), Michael discovered that he need not be miserable by holding on to his past patterns of thinking and behaving. Within months he applied for several new jobs and finally got one, and he established a new sense of self-respect. He thus became his own counsellor, arranging occasional reunions with his counsellor to boost his progress.

If you enter long-term therapy it is still possible to engage in active-change methods yourself, but it is harder to measure the success of the therapy. You may need to be more patient when rating your progress. If you know you are making progress rather than standing still, or feeling worse, then this may be enough for you. If you feel you have been seriously damaged, for example by early childhood traumas, you may anticipate that your therapy probably will take many years of tentative progress. In this case, check with yourself that you feel you are at least on an upward curve. You may also wish to ask, however, if your progress could be more efficient. While a certain amount of emotional grieving may be helpful, therapy should also be future-oriented. It should have some bearing on your everyday life and relationships, and its promise should not be based on some mythical, forever-postponed vision of future happiness.

Add up the positive aspects of your counselling. Do you have a good, mutually respectful relationship with your counsellor? Are you working well together? Is there any evidence that changes are happening? Is the pace of change what you thought it would be? If you are convinced by your own feelings and any evidence that there is definite progress, then persist. Where there is progress, but it seems slow, discuss this with your counsellor, or consider what accounts for the slow pace and whether you can do anything to improve the situation.

9
How Do You Know When Your Counselling is Going Wrong?

Many people who enter counselling or therapy believe that the therapist always knows best, and that the process of therapy is a mystery which will become clear in time. For such people there may be a long period of waiting in which doubts about whether the counselling is working are suspended. The client might think, 'This doesn't seem to be going anywhere, but the counsellor must know best. If it really isn't working, he or she would surely let me know.'

Inevitably, therapy is characterized by the therapist being in a position of strength and power. As with many of the helping professions, the client usually knows far less about the whole business and is invariably more distressed and confused than the professional they are going to for help. Or the client may finally be receiving therapy after spending months on a waiting-list, in which case his or her hopes and needs may be great, and the inclination to question this shred of hope minimal.

Counselling and psychotherapy sometimes do go wrong, and you should be aware of the possible pitfalls. Here we look at some of the areas where there may be difficulties in your counselling or therapy.

Relationship difficulties

You may be allocated to a counsellor without consultation. In some agencies you are obliged to take who you get, and it is useless to object because there are very few counsellors available, long waiting-lists, and so on. Clients have been allocated to a male counsellor when they would have preferred a woman, or to a white counsellor when they would have preferred a black counsellor. Although many organizations ask such questions at the intake stage, sometimes people are unaware that they have any right to voice such preferences. You may be too shy, afraid – or even desperate – to make your preferences known. If you know or suspect that you would rather see a counsellor of a certain race, gender, or sexual orientation, try to make this clear when you first apply for counselling. It may only become apparent after several sessions with your counsellor that you feel uncomfortable with him or her. Counsellors and therapists are only human, whatever training they may have had, and their personalities will invariably interact with yours. Although most counsellors and psycho-therapists have spent considerable time in their own therapy, this does not necessarily make them useful to everyone. Consider the following scenarios:

- Andy, a young man whose problem is glue-sniffing finds himself being counselled by an elderly, rather conservative counsellor who is interested in transpersonal therapy.

- A working-class woman, Claire, is a single parent struggling to make ends meet. On her first visit, her therapist asks her what her 'path' in life is, and whether she wishes to work on her 'deep inner processes'.

- Paul is an unemployed black man seeking help to overcome his depression. His counsellor, a white middle-class woman, begins to quiz him about his early childhood experiences.

- A highly conscientious, hard-working manager, Anne attends a therapy session to discuss problems relating to stress and finds that her therapist is a laid-back, unshaven young man who seems half asleep.

These examples show that discrepancies between people's needs, life stages, socio-economic realities, understandings of the nature of their problems, and their personalities and those of their counsellors can be glaring. These examples could be multiplied almost endlessly. There are also more subtle discrepancies between the nuances of people's interpersonal styles. You may be a basically hale-and-hearty kind of person, finding yourself with a shy and quiet counsellor; you may be somewhat reserved, and discover that your therapist is the kind of person who wants to get very close to you very quickly. We know of a case where a mature woman sought help from a counselling agency and found that her counsellor was a student, very much her junior. This relationship was not particularly productive because it was obvious that the client had much more life experience than the counsellor, who could easily have been her daughter. Furthermore, the counsellor felt acutely conscious of the discrepancy in age and maturity. Such mismatches can and do happen, although not too often. You may need to think what you would do if you were in such situations. Would you be assertive enough to ask to see another counsellor? Or would you be persistent and generous enough to make the most of the situation?

Some practitioners believe that clients can learn a great deal by working with therapists towards whom they have negative or uncomfortable feelings. If you are black you may, for example, be helped to vent your anger towards white people at your white counsellor, or, if female, your anger at men against a male counsellor. You may learn more about yourself from the apparently aloof counsellor who reminds you of your father than from the warm, caring counsellor who reminds you of your mother. You do not have to *like* your counsellor to benefit from counselling, but neither should you think that your counselling must be working because you feel extremely uncomfortable! Be aware of your own feelings about your counsellor, voice them if you can, and, after discussing it with your counsellor, reserve the right to change to another counsellor if you wish.

Other kinds of relationship difficulties can arise. Even when there is initially a good bond between you and your therapist, things can drift or change. Sometimes the bond can be 'too good', and an untherapeutic, comfortable relationship can develop. If you look forward tremendously to seeing your therapist, yet nothing much is really changing in your life, this can be a sign of a relationship which is not really therapeutic. Or your therapist may encourage you to say freely what you feel about her, on the understanding that what you say is largely 'transference' to be interpreted, yet such dynamics can sometimes go awry, and you may find yourself thinking interminably unhelpful thoughts about the therapist. Nobody enters therapy in order to develop yet another problematic or preoccupying relationship, but this sometimes occurs. If you spend a great deal of time being fascinated with, or resenting or hating, your therapist, ask yourself if this is truly therapeutic in the short or long term.

Although counsellors' supervision and personal therapy should identify and reduce or eliminate any unhelpful reactions to their clients, this is not a foolproof system. Just as you may without knowing it idealize your counsellor or try to sabotage his or her efforts, so counsellors too can have unconscious feelings towards their clients which are not helpful. Sometimes clients accurately sense this, and attempt to alert their counsellors with various signs of their discomfort or fear. If you think your counsellor is misunderstanding you, not hearing you clearly, or in any way is diverging from what you feel is what is important, make every effort to voice your feelings in one way or another. In this way you may be helping both yourself and your counsellor to become aware that there is a problem.

Sexual and emotional abuse

As far as we know there is now complete agreement among all counselling and psychotherapy organizations that *any kind of sexual contact between practitioners and their clients is unethical.* Many professional organizations insist on a lifetime ban on sexual contact, and some suggest a certain cooling-off period, for example a three-month period after counselling is terminated, during which there should be no sexual contact. Such policies have become necessary because powerful emotional and sexual feelings can surface within the therapeutic relationship, and a number of practitioners have taken advantage of these feelings.

Many people come into counselling with emotional problems relating to interpersonal traumas and loneliness. Quite naturally many see their therapists as warm, caring, loving people with whom they would like to form close relationships, and even sexual partnerships. People who have been starved of affection in their childhood may yearn for emotional fulfilment, expressing this in a belief that they are in love with their therapists. It is the therapist's task in such cases to help their client to resolve their original emotional deprivation, rather than to add to the client's problems. Some people who have been sexually abused as children may unconsciously recreate abusive situations in adult life, for example by trying to seduce caring figures.

Therapists, themselves being human and sometimes emotionally or sexually unfulfilled or unscrupulous, may fall in love with or seduce a client without any signal or invitation. In the therapeutic situation, two people spend a great deal of time alone together, with many intimate thoughts and feelings being expressed. It would be surprising if there were no emotional or sexual stirrings whatsoever. Some clients have been persuaded by their therapists that sex will enhance their therapeutic progress, or liberate them from their inhibitions. The clients may have assumed that the therapist must be right, or perhaps realized that it is wrong, but been too afraid to complain.

Over the last few years, it has become apparent that a number of clients have been sexually abused by their therapists and counsellors. It has been calculated, as a result of anonymous American surveys, that about 10 per cent of clients in therapy and counselling in the United States may have engaged in sex with their therapists. Possibly a similar statistic exists for priests, doctors, teachers, and others in positions of trust and responsibility. (By sexual abuse we refer to any sexual contact, which is clearly prohibited by all professional codes of behaviour. Sexual abuse in this context implies that the therapist or counsellor has engaged in sexual fondling or intercourse, either in the counselling room or in other settings. Even when the client has initiated or consented to sex, this is considered unethical, and as an abuse of trust and power.)

Especially if you are female, you may begin to realize that things are going wrong if your therapist frequently encourages you to talk about any erotic feelings you have for him and if he seems aroused by such talk. If he suggests physical contact, or hugs or touches you when it feels inappropriate to you, *then tell him so*. All therapists and counsellors are trained to attempt to be as objective as possible; your therapist should therefore not be personally offended if you speak your mind. If you are strongly attracted to your therapist, and are having sexual fantasies about him or her, consider whether this is part of your therapy or an obstacle to it. Discussion of your sexual fantasies or feelings may be beneficial. Again, if your therapist reacts in an inappropriate manner to what you say, make every effort to say so. If you have made a contract with your therapist, including reference to the contents of professional codes of ethics, it will be crystal clear from the beginning that sex of any kind is professionally taboo. If you have any complaints, the Prevention of Professional Abuse Network (POPAN) aims to hear such complaints and act on them. (Their address is given at the back of this book.)

Counsellors and therapists should not flirt with you, or

encourage you to think you might develop a close personal relationship with them outside or after counselling. The warmth that counsellors provide is given for therapeutic purposes only, and is not intended to make you believe that they want you as a friend.

For good theoretical reasons, certain practitioners believe they must remain rather distant, never shake hands, or indulge in similarly intimate behaviour. You must judge for yourself whether such an approach feels right for you. Some counsellors, however, may be distant and cold because that is their habitual manner, or because they are experiencing difficulties in their own lives. If warmth or care and encouragement is being withheld, ask yourself and your counsellor why, and whether this is helpful or unhelpful for you.

Certain styles of counselling or therapy may be more deliberately challenging than others. In rational emotive behaviour therapy, Gestalt therapy, primal therapy, intensive short-term dynamic psychotherapy, and encounter groups, clients are often subjected to vigorous, and even harsh, confrontation. However, extremes of confrontation are more likely to be associated with individuals than with therapeutic approaches. If you know that certain counsellors have a reputation for being aggressive or rude, think twice before entering counselling with them. If your counsellor becomes excessively aggressive, rude, or sarcastic with you, point this out to him or her. *Do not hesitate to terminate counselling if such behaviour continues.* One of the problems with intimidating therapists is that you can become too intimidated to leave when you should. If your therapist suggests that you would be 'running away from reality' by terminating therapy, think about the truth of this, and perhaps discuss it with others. Your therapist may be right, or they may simply be domineering. You are the only one who can judge what is the right balance of challenge and safety for you.

Standing still, getting worse

Many ex-clients have reported experiences of being in lengthy therapy which has failed to help them, or has even led to deterioration (Dinnage, 1988; Striano, 1988). You may form a strong attachment to a therapist and continue to see them year after year in spite of an absence of significant change or understanding; you may be lulled into a sense of security by the very ritual of regular appointments with a consistent figure in your life. Therapy can become an empty habit, or even a refuge from the real world. It is little wonder that those who hang on to their therapy as if to stave off the necessity of having to deal with an imperfect and sometimes cruel world may fail to get much from their therapy except a haven.

Clients may sense they have lost direction, or things have become stale, unchallenging, or circular. Their therapist, however, may persuade them that the current impasse must be worked through, or that the light is just at the end of the tunnel. Therapists do not hang on to their clients for the fees they pay. Counsellors and therapists believe in what they are doing, and that change takes a long time because it is a process that cannot be hurried. But they can be wrong. They may not be aware of new techniques, they may refuse to consider that approaches other than theirs could be better for certain clients in certain circumstances, and so on. Sometimes therapists may unconsciously wish to maintain a steady stream of paying clients who do not cause them too much trouble; without realizing it, they may lose their original enthusiasm and concern. Sometimes therapists become emotionally attached to their clients and do not want to let them go.

For various reasons, you may find that you make little progress. One of our interviewees said, for example, that he just kept on hoping and hoping, and also became afraid that he would be letting his therapist down if he terminated before she agreed that it was a good time to do so. Critics from within the therapeutic professions are aware that clients sometimes inadvertently end up taking care of their therapists. People have been known to persevere with therapy for ten years or more in the hope that there would ultimately be a breakthrough for them.

How can you decide when things are not going to improve simply by persevering and hoping? Exactly how long progress may take depends on the nature of your original problems; unfortunately, you cannot foretell how long is needed. Some people say, for example, that they had not realized how serious and entrenched their problems were until they had been in therapy for two or three years. Obviously, the more severe your psychological difficulties, or the more ambitious your personal growth programme, the longer it will take. If your purpose in entering therapy or counselling is to reduce or eradicate specific anxieties, phobias, relationship problems, and so on, we suggest you think seriously about changing therapists or getting independent advice if you have made no progress within a year.

More worrying than wasting your time and money is the experience of getting worse. Initial setbacks or disappointments are to be expected as an intrinsic part of the therapeutic progress. However, what if your original problem was misunderstood or misdiagnosed? Certain psychological problems, like anxiety, sometimes stem from organic disease, yet very few counsellors or therapists are medically trained. What if exceptionally painful memories are stirred up during your therapy? Clients may find themselves re-experiencing early childhood traumas and being flooded with emotions that they may not be able to control. An inexperienced, overly aggressive or ambitious therapist may push the client into such a state without the skill or knowledge to deal with the consequences. Clients can find themselves feeling confused – and sometimes even having a psychotic breakdown.

What if apparent memories of childhood sexual abuse are retrieved, yet you feel unsure about their reality? The 'false-memory syndrome' suggests that under certain conditions some people imagine, or are encouraged by over-zealous therapists to believe, that they have been sexually abused by parents when this is not the case. Most therapists and counsellors do not mis-diagnose, force you to re-experience pain, or convince you that you have suffered from imagined traumas – but how can you safeguard yourself against such possibilities? Because counselling and therapy can be such an intense and private experience, and clients are encouraged to trust their own and their therapists' perceptions, others' views can be forgotten. Therefore, if friends comment that you seem more depressed, withdrawn, or strange since entering therapy, do not entirely rule out the possibility that they may be genuinely concerned about you, rather than intrusive or demeaning.

Economics

If you are spending a lot of money on your counselling or therapy, it is prudent to weight up the advantages. Sometimes there are better alternatives than therapy. If you enter therapy intending to have weekly sessions for a few months, and suddenly realize you have been attending three times a week for four years or more, retrace your steps. If you plan to spend all your disposable income on therapy in the belief that it is the most important thing in your life, you need to consider in advance the possibility that it may not be profitable.

Some therapists and their clients believe in therapy as a life commitment, almost a religion. You could find you have nothing else left in your life if you do not keep a balanced perspective. We have mentioned, too, the error of believing that the more money and time you spend on therapy, the better you will get: many people are helped greatly by free or low-cost, time-limited therapy. From time to time reckon up how much you have spent and are spending on therapy, and what your expenditure will be over the years. You need to satisfy yourself that the probable gains will outweigh the costs before you automatically proceed with further therapy.

Repairing the therapeutic relationship

Much of the responsibility for establishing and maintaining a healthy therapeutic relationship rightfully rests on the counsellor's shoulders. However, you too are in a position to note any problems and to alert your counsellor to them. Several people we have spoken to have told us that when things were going wrong in their therapy, they tried to let the counsellor know either directly or indirectly, but were frequently unheard or unheeded.

If you have begun counselling with a clear contract, part of it may include a regular, periodic review. It may also include the fact that you can at any time raise any queries or doubts for discussion and clarification:

Tim's counsellor agreed to help him towards eliminating his shyness by using the tasks of risk-taking between sessions. However, later his counsellor seemed to be forgetting to ask him if he was completing these tasks, and if he was becoming less shy. Instead, his counsellor was concentrating exclusively on his childhood experiences. Week after week, Tim sat silently, thinking 'This isn't what we said we'd be doing', getting more and more anxious and annoyed.

Part of your responsibility is to remind the counsellor of agreements about goals and tasks. If you do not do this, you allow things to slide, and lose your therapeutic power. Like Tim, your annoyance with your counsellor, if unspoken, may in the end cause you to finish your therapy prematurely.

Or you may sense that the bond between you changes: your counsellor may seem less interested in you than he did at first; he may seem tired and distracted, or restless and critical. The reality is that he may have changed his thoughts and feelings about you, perhaps feeling less able himself to help you, or, due to external factors completely removed from your relationship, he may become more distant, without realizing it. In theory, this should not happen, but in reality it can and sometimes does. You cannot know what is going on inside your counsellor's mind, but you can certainly let him know of your feelings, for example, 'I have the feeling that something has changed between us; you don't seem to respond to me as warmly as you did when we first met.' Now, your counsellor may interpret this in various ways, but most will allow for the possibility that the client may be right, and perhaps will respond with, 'I'm sorry, you're quite right. Something has been distracting me, and I hadn't realized it until you suggested this to me.' Counsellors are not called upon to pretend to be perfect; they should, however, be honest, and should not disguise their own fallibility by making you doubt your own perceptions.

If you receive free counselling in an organization with limited resources, it can be even more important for you to keep your counsellor on track. If you have been on a waiting-list for months, and now have, say, ten sessions at your disposal, do not let things drift. Get the most from the time by preparing yourself, noting your progress, and being ready to tell the counsellor if she or he is misunderstanding you or your goals. Without getting into unhelpful conflict, be ready to tell your counsellor firmly if she or he is missing the point, or confusing you. If things start off well, but then drift away from your original aims and needs, remind the counsellor. This may be difficult if you feel you are but a 'humble' client, but it will be a poor practitioner who dismisses your protests without a serious hearing. If you feel you need to, preface any criticisms or comments with phrases such as, 'I hope you don't mind my pointing this out, but . . .', or, 'I know you're very keen on persisting with this technique, but I really don't think it's helping me at all.'

Many personal problems stem from poor early relationships, poor examples set by parents, teachers and others, and from poor, and distorted self-images. Above all, the therapeutic situation should be one in which you have the freedom to express directly any unhappiness, including any about the relationship itself.

Therapists are trained to be aware of their feelings towards each of their clients. Some may express these feelings directly to the clients, and encourage their clients to engage in similar direct expression. Others may not tell you their feelings directly, but will certainly encourage you to express yours. For example, you might say to your therapist, 'I really didn't want to come to see you today', or, 'I feel irritated when you insist on going on about my mother.' You might want to say, 'Sometimes you don't understand what I'm trying to get at', or even, 'I wish you'd wear something other than that awful brown cardigan!'

We're not suggesting that you become gratuitously insulting, but that you try to feel free to use the therapeutic situation to say those things you may not feel able to say elsewhere; in other words, to be as honest as you possibly can. It is not only negative statements that you can try out, however. 'You've got the most beautiful eyes', or, 'I really appreciate your warmth and concern' are statements which express your positive feelings and your gratitude. Some of us may be very good at being negative, and need practice in expressing positive feelings.

Counselling can be painful. It is natural that some people withdraw from the process before it becomes painful, or as soon as there are signs that certain painful subjects may be touched upon. If you become frightened about the feelings that are emerging in you, it can be tempting to blame your counsellor, and to declare that you are leaving because things are going wrong. An honest discrimination must sometimes be made, then, between a genuinely unhelpful therapeutic relationship and your own unwillingness or inability to tolerate psychological pain.

A counsellor can tell you that you should not run away from counselling because in doing so you are only running away from your own inner pain. You might think to yourself that you may choose to share your pain with a counsellor in whom you have confidence, rather than with one you cannot trust. Sensitive counsellors will not push you beyond your level of psychological endurance, even though they may confront you at times. If you experience profound emotional distress, which feels like it is being made worse by further counselling, try to discuss with your counsellor strategies for handling it. These may include temporarily working on other issues, trying other approaches, staying with the pain, or even discontinuing counselling for a while. On occasion counsellors need to be very firm with their clients, but most counsellors are flexible and will respond to individual needs.

A sense of unease or dissatisfaction with counselling may arise at any time. At such points in the process of therapy you can talk yourself out of committing yourself quite easily. There may, however be real problems, so it is wise to consider asking yourself certain questions before withdrawing prematurely. You should also discuss these questions with your therapist, if you feel able to.

- Can I relate sufficiently well to this counsellor? Do I feel understood and respected?
- Am I confident that this counsellor is competent to deal with my concerns?
- Are there any obstacles at the moment between us that cannot be discussed? What are they?
- Are the advantages of continuing counselling greater than the disadvantages? Am I really gaining something from counselling?
- Are there any danger signals about our relationship?
- Is the counselling going on longer than I expected it to?
- Do I have any way of getting outside feedback about whether I am changing or progressing in counselling?
- Has counselling drifted away from my original needs and goals?
- If not at present, does my counsellor need to instigate periodic reviews of our progress?
- Am I being honest with myself about whether I need more or less counselling?
- Do I want to try and resolve all my concerns now, or some now and others in another counselling contract?
- Where can I get advice if I feel I have been abused?

Part of the etiquette of counselling is that you are expected not to consult two or more counsellors at the same time, except, perhaps, at the stage of deciding on a counsellor to work with. It is always best to air any doubts or concerns you may have about the counselling with your counsellor in the first instance. If you feel your counsellor invariably interprets, distorts, or ignores your complaints or doubts, try to discuss this with your counsellor and consider either withdrawing as soon as possible or consulting another person, whether a friend or professional.

Counsellors and therapists are supervised in order to keep on track and to help you as best they can. You can help to 'supervise' your counsellor by being honest with him or her. If your therapist uses a tape recorder, you can ask to hear any recordings made, so that you can point out what has been especially helpful or unhelpful.

Finally, you may wish to consult another professional if you find that you are getting worse during the course of your counselling. Certainly, if a physical relationship with your therapist develops, you should stop immediately and consult another therapist.

10
What Can You Learn From Others' Experiences?

In this chapter we conclude with some examples of others' experiences of therapy, taken from our own experiences, discussions and research, and from the extensive literature on therapy and counselling. Let us begin with what is known as the question of outcome.

Does therapy work?

All counsellors and psychotherapists believe that what they are doing works, and works well. Some say that perhaps two-thirds of all clients have successful outcomes (the remaining third being dissatisfied, getting worse, or being hard to help). Others put the figure of success higher – as high as 70 or 80 per cent.

There is, however, little agreement on what constitutes a successful outcome. If the client reports that he or she has been helped, is that a success? Many would say this is enough. Others say success cannot be measured unless there is a clear statement of original needs and goals, along with some estimate of the nature and extent of the actual problems before therapy. Critics of therapy sometimes say that it is no more effective than talking to friends, priests, or doctors, or than simply waiting for the problem to pass in time. Others sometimes claim that therapy may actually make matters worse. Ask therapists and any satisfied customers and you will obviously receive confirmation of positive outcomes; ask critics and dissatisfied customers and you will get another story altogether!

In our experience, a majority of people are helped by counselling significantly. Few have either spectacularly successful or spectacularly abysmal results. A small proportion, according to surveys, have been sexually, financially, or emotionally abused – even a small proportion is worrying, of course. Readings of clients' reports of their own experiences suggest that a small proportion have been helped dramatically: suicide has been halted, depression has ended, new careers have been started, and lives have been radically changed. In the moderate range of success there are many reports of people who have lived through crises, developed better relationships, and learned better ways of coping with everyday stress. In the moderate range of failure, one can find examples of people who believe they have achieved little progress, and have wasted time.

One psychotherapist has commented that probably something like 40 per cent of clients are significantly helped whether by an excellent or average practitioner. According to this view, many people may need no more than a sympathetic listener. Indeed, this principle is central to person-centred counselling in particular: provided clients receive high levels of acceptance, empathy, and genuineness, they will be significantly helped. According to this view, almost all psychological problems benefit from a relationship-based approach.

This brings us into the debate about the effectiveness of competing approaches. Does every school of therapy produce equally successful results? If researchers were able to demonstrate convincingly the superiority of one or two approaches over all others, this would of course help consumers to make up their minds. Because of the dearth of conclusive research results in this area, it is speculated that it is the relationship between client and counsellor that is the crucial element in successful therapy.

Another debate concerns the question of whether there are particularly successful approaches for particular psychological problems. Unfortunately, most practitioners are so loyal to and enthusiastic about their own approach that they usually claim that it is equally successful with all problems and concerns. There is some research and clinical evidence that phobias and obsessions may be more successfully treated by behaviour therapy; eating disorders may require at least some elements of behaviour therapy; depression and anxiety may respond more rapidly and effectively to cognitive therapy; search for the meaning of life may be more suited to existential counselling; bereavement may be helped more by the person-centred approach; and so on.

This is a contentious subject, and many practitioners would disagree with what is written here, but as a consumer you need to know whether there are such indications. You may well wish to ask your therapist what his or her views on and experience about this are.

Mark's experience

We will now give an example of one person's experience of therapy as an illustration of some of these points.

Mark had read about a new and dramatic form of therapy and decided to travel abroad to undergo it at the founder's institute. The approach centred on the remembering and re-experiencing of emotionally painful life events. Because it was a 'tough' approach, a great deal of money was demanded in advance so that clients would not flee at the first distress, but would commit themselves to going all the way.

Mark had had all sorts of fantasies about this therapy, based on the spectacular accounts he had read. He was, he thought, an informed consumer. However, although he did indeed experience some dramatic feelings in his therapy, the reality fell short of his expectations; things did not turn out as he had hoped. It all took a lot longer than promised. The results were moderately successful in some areas of his life, and nil in others. If he complained to his therapists, he was told that he needed to have more therapy, or take more risks in his life. He met both very disappointed and very committed fellow clients, and heard both good and bad stories about their progress. When he finally decided to terminate and return home, he was quite unsure whether this was the right time. If he stayed in therapy and kept on 'feeling the feelings', would he get better? Or would he be wasting time and money?

Having paid a lot of money and travelled a long way, Mark wanted to get his money's worth. He pictured his friends at home, and recalled how he had argued with them about this therapy. His conviction about it had been total; he would find it hard to admit to any disappointment. But he was somewhat disappointed.

Some years later, reflecting back on this therapy, Mark concluded that it had been a worthwhile experience, but a qualified therapeutic success. He was unable to separate the experience of therapy from that of living in another country, and so it was difficult to evaluate changes in his life. There was no way of objectively reviewing his progress with anyone.

With the benefit of distance in time, he came to the following conclusions. In some way, perhaps the emotional experience offered by this therapy was right for him at that time in his life. In some way it had been 'unreal' because it was so removed geographically from his real, everyday life in Britain. Written accounts of the therapy had been, however well-intentioned, exaggerated and misleading. It had promised amazing results in a few months, but the reality for Mark was modest results and no end in sight. He had seen people still in this therapy for five or six years, when the promise had pointed to several months at the most. Written accounts suggested that spontaneous memories frequently erupted, whereas for most clients the whole process looked like it was far harder work than they had anticipated. There were more cognitive and behavioural aspects to it than had been written about. In its own way, it was a powerful approach, but it was not right for everyone, or for every kind of psychological problem. For Mark, it was preferable to what he saw as the slower, conversational approach devoid of strong feelings, yet if he were again to enter therapy, he would probably choose a more cognitive-behavioural approach; he would want to get on with his life rather than excavating old memories and feelings.

People who found new schools of therapy, and many therapists, are uncritically enthusiastic about their approach, and this very enthusiasm may attract clients. Consumers should think twice before throwing themselves into any particular therapy. Of course, many of us prefer to be guided by our feelings. If we read or hear about something new and dramatic that feels right for us, nothing will stop us from getting involved. This is not to say that new approaches may not have a lot to offer, because there is still, surely, much to be discovered. This story should not lead to the conclusion that only long-established, conventional approaches are to be trusted.

Ann's experience

Ann was a woman in her 30s, who reported that she had had a difficult childhood followed by stormy relationships in adult life, including two divorces. She was an energetic person, with a liking for the arts. She tended to follow her feelings, but her everyday life was often in chaos. Sometimes she drank far too much, often she felt depressed, and usually she was unemployed and might spend half the day in bed. Finally, Ann felt it had all gone too far and she sought help.

The first therapist she went to seemed kindly but uninspiring, and she soon ended the therapy. She began to read about different approaches to therapy and to ask friends about their experiences. Someone suggested that she consult a therapist living some miles away, but who had an excellent reputation. When Ann first met him, she felt put off by his apparent affluence: how could someone like him, living in great comfort, possibly understand *her*, living as she was in near poverty? Ann overcame these initial doubts, and decided to give the therapist a chance to prove himself.

The therapist confronted Ann about the way she was living her everyday life: she was wasting her talents and surrounding herself with reminders of how little she thought of herself. With her therapist's somewhat relentless challenging, Ann began to change her lifestyle. The therapist was tough and realistic enough to see that Ann had to begin by making concrete changes before doing any significant soul-searching. While his fees were not low, although initially he took her on for less than his normal rate, as Ann progressed she spontaneously felt that she wanted no charity, and accordingly she found whatever jobs she could get, lived frugally but sensibly. In this way she was able to afford to see the therapist twice a week, which for many months she found necessary. She remained in therapy with him for several years, with some gaps in between, and finally felt strong enough to end. Her life was quite different, she began a serious career, and reported a high degree of satisfaction with this therapy.

In this case, the client did a certain amount of her own research and was given good advice on who to consult. She did not terminate this therapy as soon as she sensed some dislike of her therapist, but stayed with it. Her therapist, although trained in one particular approach, had the wisdom, life-experience and common sense to understand that Ann needed to restore a sense of order and self-respect in her life before even beginning to examine the past, the subtleties of her inner life, or plans for the future. He was flexible enough to adjust his fees, and Ann was appreciative enough, and learned enough self-respect, to want to pay her way and continue the therapy. There was clearly a strong bond between them, and therapy continued for some years because the extent of Ann's problems warranted it. She was prepared to put up with some hardship because she instinctively recognized that her relationship with him was going to be significantly life-changing.

Both these examples focus on people who are resourceful enough to have read about counselling and therapy and who are unencumbered by multiple problems, dependents, and so on. All too often people end up on long waiting-lists, being given medication or forms of therapy about which they have little or no choice. Accounts of clients' experiences often make the following points: counselling and therapy is not explained to them; informed consent is not taken seriously; some advice would be appreciated; greater active participation on the part of the counsellor is wanted; and warmth, interest, and concern are always helpful (Oldfield, 1983; Howe, 1993).

Unfortunately, people using free services may feel, and may be, at the mercy of the counsellors and therapists working in those services. Some research shows, for example, that many therapists have far greater aspirations for their clients than the clients themselves. Often clients appreciate the simple opportunity to talk, to be valued, and to resolve an immediate crisis – while many therapists are wedded to the idea that amazing techniques must be tried out, or that the psychological depths of clients' minds must be plumbed. Sometimes therapists dismiss clients' pressing concerns as only hiding the 'real' issues beneath. For many people the problem which they present to their therapists *is* the problem they want to resolve. Often clients expect to attend counselling for one, two, or a few sessions, while counsellors more often prefer working at least several weeks or months with each client.

Linda's experience

Linda, in her early 20s, was experiencing panic attacks, and was referred to a student counselling service, where she was seen by an elderly female therapist. She felt quickly that there was unlikely to be any rapport between them; she also found the counselling centre cold and unwelcoming, and the therapist too seemed cold and emotionally distant. When Linda tried to voice these observations, the therapist interpreted them. Something in Linda, she suggested, had to dislike and spoil the opportunity she was being given for help. Linda found this unhelpful, but because she had no access to alternative counselling, she tried to understand and to believe what the therapist was getting at. However, she came to feel she was working far too hard to understand the therapist, and even to gratify the therapist, instead of being able to express and explore her own real difficulties.

In this case, the therapist was probably overly attached to her particular approach, and too inflexible to adapt to Linda's needs. The danger of this is that the client can be made to feel even worse about herself, something we also saw in the example of Mark. Fortunately, in Linda's case she was resolute enough to end her therapy and eventually seek an alternative.

Something to be learned from this account and others is that many clients instinctively sense when a counsellor or therapist is not right for them. 'I knew right away' is a comment we have heard quite often. Unfortunately, a bad first experience of therapy or counselling can put some people off altogether. Many clients, however, try and try again. You may be lucky enough the first time, but it is quite common for people to terminate their therapy after one or a few sessions, or even after many months, and to try again.

Many of the people we interviewed either had had previous experiences in therapy, or were intending to seek further therapy with other practitioners. Sometimes this was occasioned by dissatisfaction, and sometimes by a recognition that one helper is right for one stage in our life, and another for a later stage. You can get a vivid sense of what it is like to move from one therapist to another, or to face the need to shop around, by viewing videotapes of therapists in action. Videotapes of Carl Rogers, Fritz Perls, Albert Ellis and others have been made, for example, which show the same client with each therapist and include her comments on what she found most and least helpful. The British Association for Counselling can supply you with a list of such videos, which may be purchased or hired.

Consider the research on clients who delay help-seeking. There is some evidence that people with serious phobias often try to hide their problems and put off asking for help for as long as possible, even years, by which time the phobia is well and truly entrenched. People who are involved in violent or horrific incidents often develop post-traumatic stress disorder, partly because they refuse help, or deny they need help at the time of the incident. It is well known that when grief is not expressed serious depression can result.

The lesson from these examples is that it usually pays off to seek help without too much delay. Our own view is that you would be wise to ask for help when you first sense that something is wrong and that it is beyond your abilities to cope with it. Unfortunately, sometimes people mention to their doctors or other professionals that they are feeling depressed or anxious and are fobbed off with pills or empty reassurances. If you believe that you need help or would like to discuss sensitive personal issues, respect yourself enough to reach out for what is right for you.

Summary

Counselling and psychotherapy is a complex field to understand, and we hope that you are now somewhat clearer about the issues involved. If you find it all very confusing, it is not your failing! The confusion may often be attributed to the large array of brand names and competing professions. You can either assume that there are good counsellors trading under all sorts of banners, or you can research the subject by reading and talking to other consumers. Do not feel you must read every available account of therapy before trying it; there is far too much literature for any one person to digest! Do not become so obsessed by the idea that you have to locate the perfect therapist that you put off getting help indefinitely; there is no perfect therapist. There are probably very few brilliant therapists, but there are many highly skilled and ethical practitioners. Perhaps there is a small number of charlatans, and obviously you will want to steer clear of them.

However desperate you may be, we caution you against responding to leaflets pushed through your door which promise instant cures, dramatic relief, or ecstatic states of consciousness. When you are in great distress, *always see your GP first or talk to trusted friends, or consult organizations like the Samaritans, or others with established reputations.* We have seen leaflets and posters which can easily persuade unwary people to part with their money. Some of this literature is very impressive, detailing the many symptoms that can be cured, the apparently prestigious qualifications of practitioners, and even the offer of a free first session. But some of the more established organizations also produce literature which promises or suggests that their practitioners can deal with almost anything. Remember that they are all in business and need clients.

If you are not utterly desperate, but have a little time and the means to research what may be best for you, then delay getting immediate help until you are aware of the issues. Ask yourself who will be the best therapist or counsellor for me, at this time for my present concerns, in my present circumstances? What compromises might I need to make? (Where you live, the amount of time and money you can afford, are some of the factors to take into account.)

It is essential to think about what you want from counselling. The less clear you are, the more your counselling is likely to go astray. If you can agree at least tentatively with your counsellor on what your initial goals are, then there is a greater chance of success.

You need to have a good-enough relationship with your counsellor, which includes the freedom to express doubts and repair problems between you. You need to understand explicitly what your own goals are, and to ensure that the counsellor does not unwittingly impose his or her own goals on you. You need, too, to understand and be able to benefit from the approach used by your counsellor: far too often clients put up with treatment that they do not understand or assume they have no right to question. Whether you are paying directly for counselling or psychotherapy or receiving it as a free service, *you have the right to be treated as an intelligent, decision-making adult*. We do not want to encourage you to become a litigious malcontent or obsessive consumer researcher, but rather to alert you to pitfalls so that you choose wisely and negotiate with your counsellor assertively.

Finally, let us wish you well in your quest for happiness, greater mental well-being, or personal growth. We know that there are many benefits to be found in good counselling and psychotherapy, in spite of the fact that you may have to negotiate an obstacle course before getting the help that is effective for you. Do persist, and remember that the majority of counsellors and psychotherapists are people of integrity, who will want to help you get the best for yourself. It is worth considering, too, that professionals in this field need to know your real needs and dissatisfactions too if they are to continue to change and to refine the way they work, in order to continue to help the people they wish to help – people like you.

Appendix 1
Opinions about psychological problems questionnaires

There are four questions in this appendix. Questionnaires A and B ask about how you view the *causes* of your problems, Questionnaires C and D ask how you think these problems can be *helped*.

Causes of psychological problems

Questionnaire A

People have different views about what causes psychological problems. The following questions ask for your opinion of the causes of your *own* problems. There are no right or wrong answers: your own opinion is what counts. Please indicate how much you agree or disagree with each statement by using the following scale. Circle one number for each statement.

Disagree Strongly	Disagree Moderately	Disagree Mildly	Agree Mildly	Agree Moderately	Agree Strongly
−3	−2	−1	+1	+2	+3

My problems are caused by	Disagree Strongly	Disagree Moderately	Disagree Mildly	Agree Mildly	Agree Moderately	Agree Strongly
1 Feelings that are buried out of sight.	−3	−2	−1	+1	+2	+3
2 Illogical beliefs.	−3	−2	−1	+1	+2	+3
3 Other people not accepting me for who I am.	−3	−2	−1	+1	+2	+3
4 Becoming too anxious in certain situations.	−3	−2	−1	+1	+2	+3
5 A disorder of the brain or nervous system.	−3	−2	−1	+1	+2	+3
6 Worrying too much about what other people think of me.	−3	−2	−1	+1	+2	+3
7 Exaggerating the importance of things that may happen.	−3	−2	−1	+1	+2	+3
8 Unemployment or an unsatisfactory job.	−3	−2	−1	+1	+2	+3
9 Events that happened in childhood.	−3	−2	−1	+1	+2	+3
10 Having learnt bad habits over the years.	−3	−2	−1	+1	+2	+3
11 An inherited physical cause.	−3	−2	−1	+1	+2	+3
12 Repeating old patterns in relationships with other people.	−3	−2	−1	+1	+2	+3

My problems are caused by	Disagree Strongly	Disagree Moderately	Disagree Mildly	Agree Mildly	Agree Moderately	Agree Strongly
13 Hiding feelings from friends or family.	−3	−2	−1	+1	+2	+3
14 Lack of money.	−3	−2	−1	+1	+2	+3
15 Running away from responsibilities.	−3	−2	−1	+1	+2	+3
16 Repressing basic human impulses.	−3	−2	−1	+1	+2	+3
17 Thinking about myself too much.	−3	−2	−1	+1	+2	+3
18 Having learnt the wrong reactions to certain situations.	−3	−2	−1	+1	+2	+3
19 Unsatisfactory means of transport.	−3	−2	−1	+1	+2	+3
20 Not paying attention to my feelings.	−3	−2	−1	+1	+2	+3
21 Making harsh judgements of myself.	−3	−2	−1	+1	+2	+3
22 A lack of will power.	−3	−2	−1	+1	+2	+3
23 Not accepting myself for who I am.	−3	−2	−1	+1	+2	+3
24 Conflicting feelings about my parents when I was young.	−3	−2	−1	+1	+2	+3
25 Dissatisfaction with the community I live in.	−3	−2	−1	+1	+2	+3

My problems are caused by	Disagree Strongly	Disagree Moderately	Disagree Mildly	Agree Mildly	Agree Moderately	Agree Strongly
26 Not having a realistic view of the good and the bad things that have happened.	−3	−2	−1	+1	+2	+3
27 Conflicts in my unconscious mind.	−3	−2	−1	+1	+2	+3
28 Illness, such as colds or flu.	−3	−2	−1	+1	+2	+3
29 The state of the economy.	−3	−2	−1	+1	+2	+3
30 Unrealistic thinking.	−3	−2	−1	+1	+2	+3
31 Rewards or punishments received in the past.	−3	−2	−1	+1	+2	+3
32 A conscience that won't let me alone.	−3	−2	−1	+1	+2	+3
33 Not liking myself.	−3	−2	−1	+1	+2	+3
34 Having unrealistic expectations.	−3	−2	−1	+1	+2	+3
35 Something going wrong with my body.	−3	−2	−1	+1	+2	+3
36 Not understanding what I really feel inside.	−3	−2	−1	+1	+2	+3
37 Laziness.	−3	−2	−1	+1	+2	+3
38 Not having learnt the right ways to cope with certain situations.	−3	−2	−1	+1	+2	+3

My problems are caused by	Disagree Strongly	Disagree Moderately	Disagree Mildly	Agree Mildly	Agree Moderately	Agree Strongly
9 Not being true to myself.	−3	−2	−1	+1	+2	+3
10 Other people being unreasonable.	−3	−2	−1	+1	+2	+3
11 Putting myself down for no reason.	−3	−2	−1	+1	+2	+3
12 Poor housing.	−3	−2	−1	+1	+2	+3
13 The wrong balance of chemicals in my body.	−3	−2	−1	+1	+2	+3
14 Bad luck or fate.	−3	−2	−1	+1	+2	+3
15 Having learnt wrong ways of doing things from someone else.	−3	−2	−1	+1	+2	+3
16 Unsatisfactory relationships with other people.	−3	−2	−1	+1	+2	+3
17 It's impossible to explain the cause of my problems.	−3	−2	−1	+1	+2	+3

If you think there are other important causes not listed above, please add them here:

Causes of psychological problems

Questionnaire B

My problems are caused by

Psychodynamic
 1 Feelings that are buried out of sight.
 9 Events that happened in childhood.
12 Repeating old patterns in relationships with other people.
16 Repressing basic human impulses.
24 Conflicting feelings about my parents when I was young.
27 Conflicts in my unconscious mind.
32 A conscience that won't let me alone.

Humanistic/Interpersonal
 3 Other people not accepting me for who I am.
13 Hiding feelings from friends or family.
20 Not paying attention to my feelings.
23 Not accepting myself for who I am.
33 Not liking myself.
36 Not understanding what I really feel inside.
39 Not being true to myself.
46 Unsatisfactory relationships with other people.

Behavioural
 4 Becoming too anxious in certain situations.
10 Having learnt bad habits over the years.
18 Having learnt the wrong reactions to certain situations.
31 Rewards or punishments received in the past.
38 Not having learnt the right ways to cope with certain situations.
45 Having learnt wrong ways of doing things from someone else.

Cognitive
 2 Illogical beliefs.
 6 Worrying too much about what other people think of me.
 7 Exaggerating the importance of things that may happen.
21 Making harsh judgements of myself.
26 Not having a realistic view of the good and the bad things that have happened.
30 Unrealistic thinking.
34 Having unrealistic expectations.
41 Putting myself down for no reason.

Organic

5 A disorder of the brain or nervous system.
1 An inherited physical cause.
8 Illness, such as colds or flu.
5 Something going wrong with my body.
3 The wrong balance of chemicals in my body.

Social/Economic

8 Unemployment or an unsatisfactory job.
4 Lack of money.
9 Unsatisfactory means of transport.
5 Dissatisfaction with the community I live in.
9 The state of the economy.
2 Poor housing.

Naive

5 Running away from responsibilities.
7 Thinking about myself too much.
2 A lack of will power.
7 Laziness.
0 Other people being unreasonable.
4 Bad luck or fate.
7 It's impossible to explain the cause of my problems.

Help for psychological problems

Questionnaire C

People have different views about what may help psychological problems. The following questions ask for your opinion of how your *own* problems could be helped. There are no right or wrong answers: your own opinion is what counts. Please indicate how much you agree or disagree with each statement by using the following scale. Circle one number for each statement.

Disagree Strongly	Disagree Moderately	Disagree Mildly	Agree Mildly	Agree Moderately	Agree Strongly
−3	−2	−1	+1	+2	+3

A good way to help my problems would be	Disagree Strongly	Disagree Moderately	Disagree Mildly	Agree Mildly	Agree Moderately	Agree Strongly
1 Taking the attitude that I should count my blessings, rather than looking on the dark side of things.	−3	−2	−1	+1	+2	+3
2 Having an expert show me how to think in a more logical way.	−3	−2	−1	+1	+2	+3

A good way to help my problems would be	Disagree Strongly	Disagree Moderately	Disagree Mildly	Agree Mildly	Agree Moderately	Agree Strongly
3 Getting tablets to regulate my mood.	−3	−2	−1	+1	+2	+3
4 Learning to pay attention to my feelings.	−3	−2	−1	+1	+2	+3
5 Discussing the problems with someone in an honest, person-to-person way.	−3	−2	−1	+1	+2	+3
6 Understanding the childhood origins of the problems.	−3	−2	−1	+1	+2	+3
7 Having an expert teach me better ways of reacting to certain situations.	−3	−2	−1	+1	+2	+3
8 Getting medication.	−3	−2	−1	+1	+2	+3
9 Better housing.	−3	−2	−1	+1	+2	+3
10 Having an expert point out the meaning of my dreams and fantasies.	−3	−2	−1	+1	+2	+3
11 An improvement in the economy.	−3	−2	−1	+1	+2	+3

A good way to help my problems would be	Disagree Strongly	Disagree Moderately	Disagree Mildly	Agree Mildly	Agree Moderately	Agree Strongly
12 Examining, with an expert, what situations makes the problems better or worse.	−3	−2	−1	+1	+2	+3
13 Talking to an expert about my relationship with my parents when I was young.	−3	−2	−1	+1	+2	+3
14 Having someone listen to my feelings without giving advice.	−3	−2	−1	+1	+2	+3
15 Worrying less about what other people think of me.	−3	−2	−1	+1	+2	+3
16 Learning to live with the problems, rather than trying to change them.	−3	−2	−1	+1	+2	+3
17 Being shown by an expert how to change my outlook on the problems.	−3	−2	−1	+1	+2	+3
18 Learning to accept myself for who I am.	−3	−2	−1	+1	+2	+3

A good way to help my problems would be	Disagree Strongly	Disagree Moderately	Disagree Mildly	Agree Mildly	Agree Moderately	Agree Strongly
19 Taking my mind off myself.	−3	−2	−1	+1	+2	+3
20 Having medical treatment to put the chemicals of my body back into balance.	−3	−2	−1	+1	+2	+3
21 A better community to live in.	−3	−2	−1	+1	+2	+3
22 Learning the skills needed in difficult situations.	−3	−2	−1	+1	+2	+3
23 Putting my bad feelings aside, so I can feel more cheerful.	−3	−2	−1	+1	+2	+3
24 Tackling the problems in a planned, step-by-step way.	−3	−2	−1	+1	+2	+3
25 Learning to think more realistically.	−3	−2	−1	+1	+2	+3
26 Having other people change, rather than changing myself.	−3	−2	−1	+1	+2	+3
27 Having an expert teach me specific ways to change my behaviour.	−3	−2	−1	+1	+2	+3

A good way to help my problems would be	Disagree Strongly	Disagree Moderately	Disagree Mildly	Agree Mildly	Agree Moderately	Agree Strongly
28 Discovering what I really feel inside.	−3	−2	−1	+1	+2	+3
29 Deciding to 'keep a stiff upper lip'.	−3	−2	−1	+1	+2	+3
30 Talking about my feelings to someone I trust.	−3	−2	−1	+1	+2	+3
31 Learning to think differently about the problems.	−3	−2	−1	+1	+2	+3
32 Having an expert analyse my unconscious reasons for doing things.	−3	−2	−1	+1	+2	+3
33 Keeping busy, so as not to think about the problems.	−3	−2	−1	+1	+2	+3
34 Hearing from other people that I am doing well or trying hard.	−3	−2	−1	+1	+2	+3
35 Getting a satisfactory job.	−3	−2	−1	+1	+2	+3
36 Learning to judge myself less harshly.	−3	−2	−1	+1	+2	+3
37 Talking to someone who listens closely to what I'm really saying.	−3	−2	−1	+1	+2	+3

A good way to help my problems would be	Disagree Strongly	Disagree Moderately	Disagree Mildly	Agree Mildly	Agree Moderately	Agree Strongly
38 Realizing how I repeat old patterns in relationships with other people.	−3	−2	−1	+1	+2	+3
39 Deciding to 'grin and bear it'.	−3	−2	−1	+1	+2	+3
40 Getting tablets.	−3	−2	−1	+1	+2	+3
41 Getting physically fit and healthy.	−3	−2	−1	+1	+2	+3
42 Having an expert point out that how I think about myself can sometimes be wrong.	−3	−2	−1	+1	+2	+3
43 Better means of transport.	−3	−2	−1	+1	+2	+3
44 Coming to understand feelings or impulses that I'm not aware of.	−3	−2	−1	+1	+2	+3
45 Having more money.	−3	−2	−1	+1	+2	+3
46 Using will power to overcome the problems.	−3	−2	−1	+1	+2	+3
47 There's nothing that can be done to help my problems.	−3	−2	−1	+1	+2	+3

If you think there are other ways in which your problems could be helped, please add them here:

Help for psychological problems

Questionnaire D

A good way to help my problems would be

Psychodynamic
6 Understanding the childhood origins of the problems.
10 Having an expert point out the meaning of my dreams and fantasies.
13 Talking to an expert about my relationship with my parents when I was young.
32 Having an expert analyse my unconscious reasons for doing things.
38 Realizing how I repeat old patterns in relationships with other people.
44 Coming to understand feelings or impulses that I'm not aware of.

Humanistic/Interpersonal
4 Learning to pay attention to my feelings.
5 Discussing the problems with someone in an honest, person-to-person way.
14 Having someone listen to my feelings without giving advice.
18 Learning to accept myself for who I am.
28 Discovering what I really feel inside.
30 Talking about my feelings to someone I trust.
37 Talking to someone who listens closely to what I'm really saying.

Behavioural
7 Having an expert teach me better ways of reacting to certain situations.
12 Examining, with an expert, what situations make the problems better or worse.
22 Learning the skills needed in difficult situations.
24 Tackling the problems in a planned, step-by-step way.
27 Having an expert teach me specific ways to change my behaviour.
34 Hearing from other people that I am doing well or trying hard.

Cognitive

2 Having an expert show me how to think in a more logical way.
15 Worrying less about what other people think of me.
17 Being shown by an expert how to change my outlook on the problems.
25 Learning to think more realistically.
31 Learning to think differently about the problems.
36 Learing to judge myself less harshly.
42 Having an expert point out that how I think about myself can sometimes be wrong.

Organic

3 Getting tablets to regulate my mood.
8 Getting medication.
20 Having medical treatment to put the chemicals of my body back into balance.
40 Getting tablets.
41 Getting physically fit and healthy.

Social/Economic

9 Better housing.
11 An improvement in the economy.
21 A better community to live in.
35 Getting a satisfactory job.
43 Better means of transport.
45 Having more money.

Naive

1 Taking the attitude that I should count my blessings, rather than looking on the dark side of things.
16 Learning to live with the problems, rather than trying to change them.
19 Taking my mind off myself.
23 Putting my bad feelings aside, so I can feel more cheerful.
26 Having other people change, rather than changing myself.
29 Deciding to 'keep a stiff upper lip'.
33 Keeping busy, so as not to think about the problems.
39 Deciding to 'grin and bear it'.
46 Using will power to overcome the problems.
47 There's nothing that can be done to help my problems.

Appendix 2
Client progress chart

Instructions for completing the progress chart

Having agreed which goal or goals you are working on with your counsellor, use this progress chart to record your own view of progress towards goals. Write on it a specific goal. Consider each week whether you are moving towards or away from your goal (or not moving at all). Enter what scores seem appropriate to you: + 5 means that you have attained your goal (or that your original symptom or problem is gone); 5 means that matters (in relation to this specific goal) have got much worse. Scores in between indicate degrees of improvement or deterioration, as judged by you. Each week, mark your score on the chart with an *x* and discuss it with your counsellor. Remember that you are not scoring *yourself* but how much change there is in relation to your goal for change.

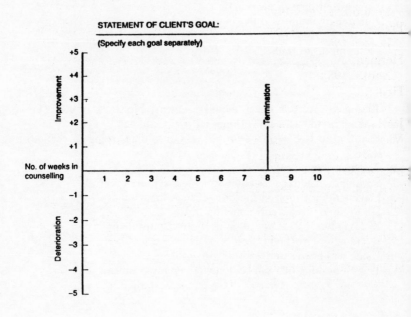

Suggested Reading

General consumer guides

Burningham, S. *Not On Your Own: The MIND Guide To Mental Health*. Harmondsworth: Penguin, 1989.

Knight, L. *Talking To A Stranger: A Consumer's Guide To Therapy*. London: Fontana, 1986.

Kovel, J. *A Complete Guide to Therapy*. Harmondsworth: Pelican, 1978.

Quilliam, S., and Grove-Stephenson, I. *The Best Counselling Guide*. London: Thorsons, 1990.

Consumers' views on counselling and psychotherapy

Dinnage, R. *One To One: Experiences of Psychotherapy*. London: Viking, 1988.

France, A. *Consuming Psychotherapy*. London: Free Association Books, 1988.

Herman, N. *My Kleinian Home*. London: Free Association Books, 1988.

Howe, D. *The Consumers' View of Family Therapy*. Aldershot, Hants: Gower, 1989.

James, J. *Room To Breathe*. London: Caliban, 1983.

Masson, J. *Final Analysis: The Making and Unmaking of a Psychoanalyst*. London: HarperCollins, 1991.

Mearns, D., and Dryden, W. (eds) *Experiences of Counselling in Action*. London: Sage, 1990.

Oldfield, S. *The Counselling Relationship: A Study of the Client's Experience*. London: Routledge & Kegan Paul, 1983.

Park, J. *Shrinks: The Analysts Analysed*. London: Bloomsbury, 1992.

Sutherland, S. *Breakdown: A Personal Crisis and a Medical Dilemma*. London: Weidenfeld & Nicolson, 1987.

Self-help

Alman, S. M., and Lambrou, P. *Self-Hypnosis: The Complete Manual for Health and Self-Change*. London: Souvenir, 1992.

Burns, D. *Feeling Good: The New Mood Therapy*. New York: Signet, 1980.

Copeland, M. C. *The Depression Workbook*. Oakland, CA: New Harbinger, 1992.

Dryden, W., and Gordon, J. *Think Your Way To Happiness*. London: Sheldon, 1991.

Ernst, S., and Goodison, L. *In Our Own Hands: A Book of Self-Help Therapy*. London: Women's Press, 1981.

Hambly, K. *Don't Be Shy*! Wellingborough, Northants: Thorsons, 1991.

Shepard, M. *Do-It-Yourself Psychotherapy*. London: Optima, 1988.

Southgate, J., and Randall, R. *The Barefoot Psychoanalyst*. London: AKHPC, 1978.

Critiques of counselling and psychotherapy

Dryden, W., and Feltham, C. (eds) *Psychotherapy and its Discontents*. Buckingham: Open University Press, 1992.

Masson, J. *Against Therapy: Emotional Tyranny and the Myth of Psychological Healing*. New York: Atheneum, 1988.

Smail, D. *Taking Care: An Alternative To Therapy*. London: Dent, 1987.

Szasz, T. *The Myth of Psychotherapy*. New York: Syracuse University Press, 1988.

Wood, G. *The Myth of Neurosis*. London: Macmillan, 1983.

General reading

Bond, T. *Standards and Ethics for Counselling in Action*. London: Sage, 1993.

Dryden, W. (ed.) *Individual Therapy: A Handbook*. Buckingham: Open University Press, 1990.

Feltham, C., and Dryden, W. *Dictionary of Counselling*. London: Whurr, 1993.

Holmes, J., and Lindley, R. *The Values of Psychotherapy*. Oxford: Oxford University Press, 1989.

Howe, D. *On Being a Client*. London: Sage, 1993.

McLeod, J. *An Introduction To Counselling*. Buckingham: Open University Press, 1993.
Yalom, I. *Love's Executioner*. Harmondsworth: Penguin, 1989.

Fiction portraying experiences of therapy

Alther, L. *Other Women*. New York: New American Library, 1985.
Perriam, W. *The Fifty-Minute Hour*. London: Paladin, 1991.
Rossner, J. *August*, New York: Warner, 1984.

| *Organizations*

It is outside the scope of this book to offer a comprehensive list of organizations, or to endorse any particular organizations. The following contact addresses are intended as a starting point in your search for appropriate counselling or psychotherapy. It is often helpful to talk to a member of staff if possible or to read through organizations' literature in order to come to decisions as to which to investigate further. Organizations such as BAC or MIND should be able to give you contact numbers for specialist agencies. Some London-based organizations may be able to refer you to regional centres. Contact addresses and telephone numbers do change periodically, so you may need to refer to directory enquiries (192) for current numbers in some cases.

British Association for Counselling   01788 550899
1 Regent Place
Rugby, Warwickshire CV21 2PJ

United Kingdom Council for Psychotherapy   0171 487 7554
Regent's College
Regent's Park
London NW1 4NS

British Psychological Society   0116 2549568
St Andrew's House
48 Princess Road East
Leicester LE1 7DR

British Association of Psychotherapists   0181 452 9823
37 Mapesbury Road
London NW2 4HJ

Association of Humanistic   0181 983 1492
Psychology Practitioners
14 Mornington Grove
London E3 4NS

Institute of Group Analysis 0171 431 2693
1 Daleham Gardens
London NW3 5BY

MIND 0181 519 2122
Granta House
15–19 Broadway
Stratford
London E15 4BQ

Prevention of Professional
Abuse Network (POPAN) 0171 794 3177
Flat 1, 20 Daleham Gardens
London NW3 5DA

Relate 01788 573241
Herbert Gary College
Little Church Street
Rugby CV21 3AP

Samaritans 01753 32713
17 Uxbridge Road
Slough SL1 1PQ

Cruse Bereavement Care 0181 940 4818
Cruse House
126 Sheen Road
Richmond TW9 1UR

Victim Support 0171 735 9166
Cranmer House
39 Brixton Road
London SW9 6DZ

Women's Therapy Centre 0171 263 6200
6 Manor Gardens
London N7 6LA

Nafsiyat 0171 263 4130
278 Seven Sisters Road
London N4 2HY

Metanoia   0181 579 2505
13 North Common Road
London W5 5HN

Westminster Pastoral Foundation   0171 937 6956
23 Kensington Square
London W8 5HN

Association of Cognitive-Analytic Therapists   0171 955 4822
Munro Clinic
Guys Hospital
London SE1 9RT

Association of Rational Emotive
   Behaviour Therapists   0121 427 7292
49 Wood Lane
Harborne
Birmingham B17 9AY

Centre for Stress Management   0181 293 4114
156 Westcombe Hill
London SE3 7DH

Norwich Centre for Personal and
Professional Development   01603 617709
7 Earlham Road
Norwich NR2 3RA

Resources

The following directories are published annually:

British Association for Counselling. Counselling and Psychotherapy Resources Directory. Rugby: BAC.

British Confederation of Psychotherapists. London: BCP.

British Psychological Society. Directory of Chartered Psychologists. Leicester: BPS.

United Kingdom Council on Psychotherapy. The National Register of Psychotherapists. London: UKCP.

Index